# MENSA OTABIL

# WISDOM

*The Foundation and Law of God's World*

# WISDOM

©2018 Mensa Otabil

All rights reserved. No part of this publication may be reproduced, stored in a retrieval system, or transmitted in any form by any means without the prior written permission of the publisher, or be otherwise circulated in any form of binding or cover other than in which it is published and without similar condition being imposed upon the subsequent purchaser.

ISBN: 9781793319210

*For enquiries contact:*

International Central Gospel Church

P.O. Box 7933

Accra-North, Ghana, West Africa

Tel: +233-302-688000 | Fax: +233-302-688007

Website: www.centralgospel.com

Email: otabil@centralgospel.com

Unless otherwise indicated, all scriptural references are from the New King James Version of the Holy Bible.

Cover Design: Oxygen

# DEDICATION

I dedicate this book to the youth of the church, particularly those in their teens and twenties. The world of our young people is a very difficult one. The pressures on them are very high. I pray this book helps them to see and to walk in the wisdom of God as they avoid the snares of today's world and righteously navigate their lives. May the parents, pastors and peers in their lives counsel them in God's wisdom, and may the Lord's wisdom be seen throughout their generation.

# ACKNOWLEDGEMENTS

I thank the Lord, my God for the inspiration and revelation of His wisdom to write this book. I thank Him for the grace over my life and for the opportunity to minister His word to His people. I also thank my wife, Joy, for her wisdom and understanding as we together continue to live out God's purposes for our lives.

Additionally, I want to thank those who contributed to the production of this book, including: Erinn Ofori as the chief editor, Nana Kwadwo Duah of Oxygen for the cover design, Invictus for the page layout and NSAB Limited for the printing.

# TABLE OF CONTENTS

DEDICATION ..................................................................................... II
ACKNOWLEDGEMENTS................................................................ III
INTRODUCTION................................................................................ 7
1. DIMENSIONS, FUNCTIONS AND TYPES OF WISDOM.................. 11
    *What is wisdom?* ............................................................................ 11
    *Five dimensions of wisdom* .......................................................... 12
    *Four functions of wisdom* ............................................................ 18
    *Three types of wisdom*.................................................................. 20
2. THE WISDOM AND MYSTERY OF GOD .......................................... 29
    *The Christmas story* ..................................................................... 31
    *The incarnation in Christ* ............................................................ 32
    *Partakers of God's wisdom*........................................................... 37
    *People God chooses* ...................................................................... 39
3. THE EXCELLENCE OF WISDOM ...................................................... 41
    *Where wisdom is found*................................................................ 41
    *Wisdom's message* ........................................................................ 44
    *Wisdom's companions* .................................................................. 48
    *Wisdom's enemies* ........................................................................ 51

*Wisdom's work* ........................................................................... 53
*Wisdom's plea* ........................................................................... 56

## 4. WISDOM VS. FOOLISHNESS .................................................. 59
*Wisdom builds* ........................................................................... 63
*Foolishness destroys* ................................................................ 66
*Become a wise builder* ............................................................. 70
*The source of foolishness* ........................................................ 71

## 5. TWO CASE STUDIES OF WISDOM: ELIHU AND BEZALEL ...... 77
*Elihu's wise observations* ........................................................ 77
*Bezalel's wisdom* ...................................................................... 80
*Wisdom and workmanship: in theory and in practice* ......... 82

## 6. SOLOMON'S WISDOM .............................................................. 89
*Solomon's peer evaluation* ...................................................... 89
*7 demonstrations of Solomon's wisdom* ............................... 95
*Solomon and the two mothers* .............................................. 102
*The destroyer's logic* .............................................................. 108
*The preserver's logic* .............................................................. 110
*Something greater* .................................................................. 113

## 7. WISDOM IN OUR LIVES ........................................................ 119
*How wisdom develops* ........................................................... 119
*The anatomy of wisdom* ........................................................ 123

## 8. HOW TO GET WISDOM ........................................................ 145
*Attracting wisdom* .................................................................. 146
*Seven ways to get wisdom* .................................................... 149

## 9. PRAYING FOR WISDOM ....................................................... 161
## ENDNOTES ................................................................................. 167

# INTRODUCTION

When God called Israel as a nation, He gave them laws such as thou shalt not commit adultery, but He did not tell them the consequences of disobeying that law. As the nation grew and lived under the laws of God, they began to observe the effects of adultery and other actions God told them not to perform. They saw the practical way in which the law of God worked in their lives and therefore built their wisdom around the application of God's word.

For example, when God said, thou shalt not bear false witness, the children of Israel saw that telling lies or spreading rumours about a person had certain destructive effects on people's reputation and on society, so they took note of this in wisdom.

**Biblical Foundations**

The foundational scriptures for this book will be from Proverbs 3:19-20; Psalms 104:24; and Psalms 19:1-3.

Proverbs 3:19-20 reads,

> *The LORD by wisdom founded the earth;*
> *By understanding He established the heavens;*

> By His knowledge the depths were broken up,
> And clouds drop down the dew.

In this context, the Bible uses the word 'heavens' to mean the universe. Therefore, the Lord founded the earth by wisdom and He established the universe by understanding.

Psalms 104:24 declares,

> O LORD, how manifold are Your works!
> In wisdom You have made them all.
> **The earth is full of Your possessions--**

Take particular note of the phrase, *in wisdom You have made them all.* Also, note that it does not say, "In physics, in chemistry, in biology, or in astrophysics, You have made them all." It says, *in wisdom.*

The scripture tells us that wisdom is what God used to create the universe and that wisdom itself is woven into the universe. This means that the laws of physics and the laws of nature are manifestations of the wisdom of God. In the universe and the laws that run it – whether it is gravity, motion or thermo-dynamics – we see the manifestations of God's wisdom because God wove the universe through wisdom. This is very important because in order to function well in God's universe, you have to understand wisdom.

Psalms 19:1-3 says,

> *The heavens declare the glory of God; and the firmament shows His handiwork.*
>
> *Day unto day utters speech, and night unto night reveals knowledge. There is no speech nor language where their voice is not heard.*

## INTRODUCTION

In Psalms19:2, it says, *day unto day utters speech, and night unto night reveals knowledge.* In other words, when you observe the Creator's order, from the earth, to the other planets in our solar system, beyond our solar system to our galaxy, and beyond our galaxy to the other galaxies in the universe, all of these express the language of God. The wisdom and order by which the universe is structured, is God speaking. The universe itself is a language of wisdom.

These are very deep and profound verses because they touch on the core significance of life; that **wisdom is the law and the language of God's universe.**

Wisdom is a very powerful force. It is not just something that helps you to make choices. It is a system, a law that runs the entire universe. Wisdom regulates life in the universe; wisdom sustains the universe; wisdom is the instrument by which God guides everything. Wisdom is the fundamental law of the universe. It is God's language. God Himself established the universe on wisdom, so we must ask God to help us expand in wisdom and understanding so we can move our lives along the path that God has called us.

In this book I will frequently reference the Wisdom Books of the Bible, which are primarily the Books of Proverbs, Ecclesiastes, Song of Solomon, Psalms and Job. The anchor however, will be the Book of Proverbs. A **proverb** is normally a very short and memorable saying, which has relevance to different situations. The Book of Proverbs in the Bible represents the collective wisdom of Israel. As Israel grew as a nation, it began to put together its wisdom. This is how any culture's wisdom develops, and they are usually captured in folktales, stories or, in the case of Israel, in proverbs.

In this book we explore manifestations, companions, dimensions, functions, types, examples and sources of wisdom. We also look at how to attract wisdom, and how to hold onto wisdom.

CHAPTER

# 01

# DIMENSIONS, FUNCTIONS AND TYPES OF WISDOM

## What is Wisdom?

If we consider that wisdom is the language of God, then defining it becomes an understandably large task. Yes, we can define wisdom according to the dictionary, and one definition it offers is *"the quality of having experience, knowledge, and good judgment; the quality of being wise."* This definition refers to two things:

- The soundness of an action or decision with regard to the application of experience, knowledge, and good judgment, or

- The body of knowledge and principles that develops within a specified society or period.[1]

Such a definition helps us to understand wisdom from a theoretical or cognitive point of view, but dictionaries still fall short of helping us comprehend the language of God and the foundation of His universe.

In order to grasp wisdom fully, the most reliable source for understanding comes from the Bible, so we will look at wisdom as it is defined in the Scriptures.

Wisdom does not have only one expression in the Bible. The Hebrews and the Greeks had slightly different approaches to wisdom. For the Hebrews wisdom was practical; to the Greeks wisdom was philosophical or abstract. In fact, the idea of philosophy itself comes from the Greeks. They valued concepts and ideas, and that is where the idea of philosophy was generated. The word philosophy itself is a combination of the Greek words *philos*, meaning love and *sophia*, meaning wisdom. Philosophy then, literally means the love of wisdom.

It is very difficult to define wisdom in one sentence so in this chapter I'm going to define wisdom from different angles. To do a thorough examination, we will look at five dimensions of wisdom, four functions of wisdom and three types of wisdom. First, let's examine the five dimensions, which I have labelled as spiritual, mental, moral, practical and governmental wisdom.

## Five Dimensions of Wisdom

### 1. The spiritual dimension of wisdom.

Psalms 111:10 says, *The fear of the LORD is the beginning of wisdom*. It is the doorway to wisdom. The fear of the Lord has two aspects. To fear the Lord means:

- To turn away from sin and everything that is wrong, and
- To reverence, or have respect for God.

The fear of the Lord can be likened to the way an electrician fears electricity. Every electrician works with electricity, but they have a healthy fear of it. They know its awesome power and before any good electrician starts a job they take all the necessary precautions because they understand the laws and principles of electricity. They don't violate those laws or principles because they know the power of electricity and what it can do. In their process of wiring they follow a strict line of order, putting the right wires and circuits in their proper places. Their carefulness is a sign of respect, but it is not the kind of respect that causes you to shy away from it altogether. It is a respect that allows you to get the job done, and at all times remember the power you are working with.

When the Bible talks about the fear of the Lord, it is also not a fear that should make you stand away from God. It is a type of respectful fear that makes you recognize the awesomeness of God and therefore causes you to conduct your life according to His principles. In the same way that the electrician works with electrical currents according to the principles that will preserve, rather than jeopardize his life, the fear of the Lord is a kind of wisdom that makes you careful to operate within God's principles.

If you don't have this first spiritual dimension – the fear of the Lord – it means you haven't even begun the journey to wisdom.

## 2. The mental dimension of wisdom.

Mental wisdom is the dimension that most people are familiar with. It is having a deep understanding or insight into how life operates.

This is different from merely having a high IQ or good grades in school. Intelligence and knowledge are close, but not the same as wisdom. For the Jews, mental wisdom was gained by observing nature. The Book of Proverbs has a lot of reference to animals such as foxes, lions, snakes, ants, bees, deer and so on. Why? Because they learn wisdom from observation and not from books. Book knowledge does not necessarily give you wisdom.

The mental aspect of wisdom is gained through observation and appreciation of how things work. You can understand gravity without really appreciating it. You can know how to do algebra without having an appreciation of how it can be useful in your life. Wisdom is when you have the insight to put knowledge to use.

In Proverbs 6:6, the sluggard – the lazy man – is told to go and observe the ant and learn. The sluggard knows the ants are marching in a straight line. He sees that they are carrying food. Where wisdom comes in is when he really looks beyond those facts and observes that they do this when there is food available, that they gather everything they can, and that they store it in their chambers. Furthermore, wise observation will lead the sluggard to notice that when food is not available, that is when they eat what they have stored. When he notices that the ants' focus, order and their seizure of the opportunity before them provides for them when there is scarcity, then he is increasing in wisdom. Once the sluggard applies this to his life and lets it inform his practices, he has acquired mental wisdom by observation. Mental wisdom is watching life in order to learn from it and improve your own.

You can gain a lot of insight by watching other people's successes and mistakes. For example, if you observe a rich man who has a decent family and seems to have everything going well for him, then suddenly decide to indulge in extra-marital affairs, just watch.

You will observe his life derailing. You will see he doesn't pay attention to himself any more, makes a lot of risky choices and soon begins to lose everything – his money, his respect, his family and finally even loses the other woman. When you observe this sequence of events you should be able to gain wisdom to apply to your own life. However, if you don't learn but also repeat it, then you will have failed the wisdom test. You don't need to personally experience issues before you learn. Just watch how that experience is affecting people and get wisdom from it.

### 3. The moral dimension of wisdom.

Moral wisdom is the ability to differentiate right from wrong. It is a moral force to exhibit righteous conduct. We often judge people's wisdom by their morality. If the person is always doing the wrong thing, making wrong choices and decisions, we don't judge them to be wise, but if the person is doing the right thing, we credit them with having wisdom. Moral wisdom is often inspired by spiritual wisdom. For example, lying, stealing and cheating are all immoral. Not only do they lead to negative practical outcomes that can be observed, like the cheating spouse whose life falls apart, they are wrong because they go against God's instructions.

### 4. The practical dimension of wisdom.

Practical wisdom is the technical aspect of wisdom. It is the ability to use one's creativity to solve problems. Most people in the Hebrew society viewed wisdom in this manner. The first person described in the Bible as having wisdom was a technical craftsman, a manufacturer.

When you view a person's life you can tell whether they have wisdom or not by the practical solutions they apply to their challenges. When I was growing up I had a friend who lived in a one-room apartment. He didn't have much except a bed and a little cupboard. Any time I visited him I noticed that his bed was neatly dressed with his food items well arranged in the cupboard – a box of cornflakes, some tins of milk, sardines, corned beef and so on. (I later learnt that all those boxes and tins were empty). His clothes were also always neatly ironed. I admired him and desired to be like him. He was not rich and did not have much, but just entering his room showed you wisdom.

Now you can enter another person's room with the same elements – cornflakes, tins of milk and sardines, clothes and all, but everything scattered all over the place and presume that there is something wrong with that person. My friend had practical solutions to his one room apartment, but there are some people with five room apartments that are nowhere as neat as my friend's was.

Whether observing an individual, a family or even a nation, you can tell when the person or group has wisdom because wisdom can be personal or collective.

If you go to a country and the bus system is running, cars are parked at the right place, food is sold by appropriate vendors and in the right setting, and items are sold in shops rather than on the pavement, you will conclude that the people of that society have wisdom.

When you enter another country that also has buses, cars, streets, pavement, food and shops, but the cars are parked haphazardly, creating traffic jams, sales are made outside the shops on the pavement and the whole environment is messy and chaotic, you will rightly conclude that collectively, these people don't display practical wisdom.

## 5. The governmental dimension of wisdom.

Continuing with the collective aspect of wisdom, governmental wisdom is the dimension that has to do with ruling a group, not only with order, like my previous example, but also ruling with fairness and equity. Usually the term 'governmental' causes people to think first of the government, however in the Hebrew society where much of the wisdom we know originated, the first governmental system was the family.

In the Book of Proverbs you see statements addressed to "my children" or "my son," or phrases like "my mother/father told me," because many of the proverbs are about how to govern your home.

Wisdom is easily seen in the way a home is governed. You can visit a home where the walls have all kinds of drawings on them, toys are scattered everywhere and the parents will attribute the untidiness to the children. Meanwhile, in another home also having children, the walls will be clean and the rooms tidy. The difference is the governmental system – how each family is organized.

You visit a family and their little children respectfully welcome you while the children of another family play all over you. This is the wisdom of both families in manifestation. For the Hebrews, wisdom was how you govern and the first place of government was the home.

Citizens of one country who live anyhow and litter indiscriminately in their own country often travel to other countries and behave differently. This is because in other countries behavior and garbage management is collectively governed. On the individual level, their desires are governed in a way and to an effect that the people wait till they get to the right place to deposit any waste. The difference between the two countries is the governmental wisdom of each environment. One is strong in governmental wisdom, while the other is weak.

Wisdom is central to the state of our lives and for the Hebrews wisdom was assessed in these five dimensions -the spiritual, the mental, the moral, the practical, and the governmental. All of which apply at the individual level as well as to the collective.

## Four Functions of Wisdom

Moving from the five dimensions or realms in which wisdom operates, let's look specifically at what wisdom does for us. One way of understanding wisdom is by its function, and to a large extent, wisdom is a conduit or a bridge from one state to another. Whether as a map, a gap, a tap or a cap, wisdom is what connects two things that may otherwise have no way of coming together.

**Wisdom is the map that moves you from where you are to your next destination.** It is like a navigation system that guides you through the changing seasons of life. As you move through life the wisdom you have will be like a map for you. When you arrive at a junction in your life don't know where to turn, wisdom will determine where you turn. It is your map. If you are confused in life and don't know where to turn, it is a deficiency in wisdom.

**Wisdom is the gap between your problems and your solutions.** Every problem in life has some form of a solution and it is our wisdom that stands between our problems and our solutions. The problems we have may be how to live a holy life, how to grow spiritually, how to get along with our spouse, how to have financial security, how to develop in our professional life, how to raise our children, how to maintain good relationships and so on. These are all problems that have solutions.

The gap between your problem and your solution is wisdom and once you settle this fact, you don't blame the problem; you simply go for the needed wisdom. This is why the Bible tells us that in our getting, we should get wisdom. Every problem we have has a solution, and that solution is available with the applicable wisdom.

**Wisdom is the tap through which your energies flow.** Everything you have – gifts, talents and abilities – is channelled through your wisdom. What would happen if you had a large reservoir of water but you channel it through a choked pipeline? There would be no flow. The problem would not be an absence of water, but a choked pipe. Wisdom is like a pipeline; when your wisdom is choked it blocks the flow of your gifts, talents and abilities.

Using the same analogy in a slightly different way, think of what would happen if you have a reservoir filled with clean water, but the pipeline is filthy. The water will be contaminated. Again, the problem would not be the purity of the water at the source, but the channel of the water is filthy so the clean water will become polluted.

You can give money to people who think their problems are financial, but they'll still be poor, because they will mismanage the money. If the pipeline that is your wisdom is filthy, everything that flows through it will be filthy. Wisdom is your tap.

**Wisdom is the cap to your performance in life.** Finally, wisdom is also like a cap. You cannot perform beyond your level of wisdom. As your wisdom is, so will your life be. Wisdom is the limit to your reality; like the cap of a bottle. Once you cap a bottle, nothing can be added to it. Your wisdom is the uppermost limit of what you can achieve. So when I find myself repeating the same cycles and facing the same problems, I have to check my wisdom.

I have observed that my life moves in three-year cycles. Every three years I have to renew myself otherwise I feel stagnant. Other people may encounter the same thing. Perhaps for you it is five years, or every year. Regardless of the specific time period, my point is that we have to regularly stretch ourselves because we need more capacity in order to continue growing. The best way to expand one's capacity is to expand one's wisdom because wisdom is the cap to our performance. When a person's wisdom is capped, nothing will improve their performance until they gain more wisdom.

There are people who have undergone all sorts of training programmes yet without any improvement in their performance. This is because they have capped their wisdom. In other words, there is a fundamental understanding that has not shifted for them and until that happens no number of seminars or training programmes can improve them. It will be a wasted venture.

## Three Types of Wisdom

In 1 Corinthians 2:1-8, the Apostle Paul talks about the focus of his ministry and he distinguishes it from other expressions that were in existence at the time. In his statement he reveals three kinds of wisdom that are important for us to recognize:

> *And I, brethren, when I came to you, did not come with Excellence of speech or of wisdom declaring to you the Testimony of God. For I determined not to know anything among you except Jesus Christ and Him crucified. I was with you in weakness, in fear, and in much trembling. And my speech and my preaching were not with persuasive words of human wisdom, but in demonstration of the Spirit and of power, that your faith should not be in the wisdom of men but in the power of God. However, we speak wisdom among those*

*who are mature yet not the wisdom of this age, nor of the rulers of this age, who are coming to nothing. But we speak the wisdom of God in a mystery, the hidden wisdom which God ordained before the ages for our glory, which none of the rulers of this age knew; for had they known, they would not have crucified the Lord of glory.*

**Human Wisdom**

The first kind of wisdom Paul describes is human wisdom, which he later also called the wisdom of this age. Human wisdom, or wisdom of this age is the wisdom has come up with from their experiences, experiments and observations. It is based on things like culture, science and philosophy. The wisdom of this age is not concerned about God or eternity, because the source of its conclusions comes only from human understanding and the limits of human capacity. The wisdom of this age is based on observation, logic, or tradition. It does not base its understanding on spiritual laws, principles or consequences.

Human wisdom is earthly; it is self-seeking and it is sensory. It is not spiritual; it does not seek to know and understand God, and it appeals to the senses, not to the spirit. Human wisdom is not necessarily evil; it has some good in it, and there are a lot of good things you can find in human culture, logic or philosophy. The difficulty with human wisdom is that it doesn't factor God in. It takes the spiritual out and it just relates to life as it is seen in the natural – by observation and by learning. It can help you to understand things to a certain degree, but it is limited. Human wisdom is a limited wisdom.

The clearest example of human wisdom in this world is found in the Book of Ecclesiastes, because it talks about wisdom without God. If you really want to see how the wisdom of this age functions, then read the Book of Ecclesiastes. Ecclesiastes 1:9 tells us that with regard to human wisdom, the bottom line is:

> *That which has been is what will be, that which is done is what will be done, and there is nothing new under the sun. What is crooked cannot be made straight, and what is lacking cannot be numbered.*

In other words, you cannot change anything. The way things are, that's the way they are and that's the way they will be. Nothing will change.

Ecclesiastes 3:19-20 says:

> *For what happens to the sons of men also happens to animals; one thing befalls them: as one dies, so dies the other. Surely, they all have one breath; man has no advantage over animals, for all is vanity. All go to one place: all are from the dust, and all return to dust.*

This is as good as it gets according to human wisdom. Culture will call it tradition. Science will call it objectivity. Philosophy will call it existentialism. They all roam in circles. Without God, human wisdom cannot think beyond the limits of intellectualism. In human wisdom intellect, observation, tradition are the bounds of its understanding. It doesn't factor God in; it doesn't have the tools to look at life beyond death; it can't observe, test, or reason with eternity. It just observes human life and concludes. *What is life? It's nothing. We are all like animals.* That is why human wisdom always concludes in the pleasures of life. Just eat, drink and wonder. Whatever your pleasure, just be happy because ultimately, you will die and return to the earth.

Ecclesiastes 7:16-17 continues to exemplify human wisdom:

> *Do not be overly righteous, nor be overly wise: Why should you destroy yourself? Do not be overly wicked, nor be foolish: Why should you die before your time?*

This is at the core of human wisdom. It says don't do too much; just serve God a little and be happy in the world a little. Just be a nice person. Why do you want to bother yourself? Has anyone ever asked you, *why do you go to church all the time? Or why do you refer to the Bible so much? Don't you think you are over-doing it?* What their questions illustrate is the logic of human wisdom. It says, a little here, a little there; balance and moderation is the key to life. Just try to be a good person, don't offend anyone, stay in the middle, don't rock the boat and you will be fine. Your response should be to ask them, *the key to which life?* Because balance, moderation, and playing the middle, certainly are not the key to eternal life. Not even being a good, decent person will earn you eternal salvation.

Human wisdom tries to find a space where you can enjoy everything and not be accountable to God. So Paul says, when I came to you I didn't come to you in human wisdom. There is some good in human wisdom but it has its flaws. Human wisdom is not the ultimate of wisdom.

**Demonic Wisdom**

The second kind of wisdom mentioned in 1 Corinthians 2:1-8 is demonic wisdom. Demonic wisdom is what Paul describes as *the wisdom of the rulers of this age.* Some biblical scholars believe that the phrase 'rulers of this age' refers to political leaders, powerful people or governmental leaders. I can understand that perspective, but I believe 'rulers of this age' refers to demonic entities and I'll tell you why. My view is based on a clear contrast that is made in verse 6 where it says:

> *However, we speak wisdom among those who are mature yet not the wisdom of this age, nor of the rulers of this age, who are coming to nothing.*

Pay close attention to the interjection of the word, 'nor.' 'Nor' is a conjunction that introduces a second part to a statement. For example, you might say, *I neither like this nor that*. You could not be speaking about the same thing because one is contrasted with the other. There have to be two separate items you are distinguishing. In Paul's case, he distinguishes *the wisdom of this age* with something else - *the rulers of this age*. He's letting us know that the two are not the same.

When you read Ephesians 6:12, it says,

> *For we do not wrestle against flesh and blood, but against principalities, against powers, against the rulers of the darkness of this age, against spiritual hosts of wickedness in the heavenly places.*

Flesh and blood is one thing. It refers to human beings. But principalities, powers, the rulers of the darkness of this age and spiritual hosts of wickedness in heavenly places, well those are demonic entities. Paul clarifies that yes, there is human wisdom of this age, but there is something else. There is the wisdom of the rulers of this age, particularly of the darkness of this age. For human wisdom, their 'god' so-to-speak is, tradition, logic, education, reason, intellect, etc. 2 Corinthian 4:3-4 goes on to tell us who is the god of the wisdom of the rulers of this age. It says,

> *But even if our gospel is veiled, it is veiled to those who are perishing, whose minds the god of this age has blinded, who do not believe, lest the light of the gospel of the glory of Christ, who is the image of God, should shine on them.*

The 'god of this age' is Satan. Therefore the wisdom of the rulers of this age is demonic wisdom. There is such a thing as demonic wisdom. It is wisdom that is antagonistic to God. Unlike human wisdom, which simply doesn't factor God in and cannot reason on a spiritual level, demonic wisdom actively fights God Himself and everything that He has created and established.

We see so much of that wisdom prevalent in our world today. It fights the institution of marriage, it fights the fundamental differences between male and female, it is propagated by a very intelligent, well-educated people but everything it does is to lie against the truth of God and to undermine the Word of God. It is the wisdom of the rulers of this age, so don't ever assume that because somebody has a doctorate every opinion they have is right.

Remember, human wisdom is natural. It is inferior to the supernatural and is subject to the influence of the spiritual. A smart person can be a puppet for the devil, because a person of human wisdom reasons with a natural tool, their brain. But the devil operates with powers, principalities, and wickedness, which are spiritual tools. Just because somebody has a world-class education doesn't mean everything they say is validated by God. Some of the most respected philosophers and scientists of this world have worked their intellect, even masterfully, to justify and rationalize all sorts of things that are not right.

Let me just be straight and say that a lot of people of that caliber are used by the rulers of this age to propagate ideas that are antagonistic to God. Sometimes I see Christians quote and adopt role models who have achieved a lot in life by human standards. It is great to have successful entrepreneurs, famous business leaders and brilliant inventors as role models – to a certain extent. We can learn a lot from their lives but we have to be very careful because some of the wisdom they speak is not of God; its source comes from the rulers of the darkness of this world. These role models, sometimes knowingly and sometimes unknowingly put out ideas into the world that if you are not careful you can buy into them and they will challenge your Christian commitment to God.

## Godly Wisdom

After Paul talks about demonic wisdom and human wisdom, he then tells us about the third kind of wisdom, that is, godly wisdom, and he calls godly wisdom the hidden wisdom. Why does the Bible call godly wisdom hidden? Does it mean that God doesn't want us to find wisdom? No, it means that it is protected from the corruption of this world. Godly wisdom is wisdom that has neither been corrupted by men nor by Satan. God's wisdom is very simple on the outside, but very deep on the inside. It is hidden in simplicity so that even a child can find it. Let's look at how Jesus described the wisdom of God in Matthew 11:25,

> *At that time Jesus answered and said, "I thank You, Father, Lord of heaven and earth, that You have hidden these things from the wise and prudent and have revealed them to babes."*

Godly wisdom is spiritually discerned; it is not something you can get through logic or from a university degree. Your ancestors cannot pass it down to you. The scientific method cannot create a formula for it. God's wisdom is eternal. It won't say that Pluto is a planet for decades, then change the story and downgrade it to a star. That sounds like somebody got it wrong, either back then or maybe now. That wisdom cannot be the ultimate. Godly wisdom is pure. It is the absolute truth. It doesn't change and cannot be disproven. It isn't convoluted. It is simple. Jesus says even babes can have it revealed to them.

So we have three kinds of wisdom: human wisdom, demonic wisdom and godly wisdom. As humans, we operate a lot by human wisdom. When you listen to musicians, Ghanaian highlife music for example, you will hear a lot of good human wisdom. When you read books, you will find good human wisdom. Sometimes you listen to great speakers, who share a lot of useful, valuable human wisdom. Human wisdom is good but it is not perfect, because it only looks at life from the earthly plane. You should have human wisdom, but you shouldn't limit yourself to it.

Demonic wisdom is simply wrong. It is evil. It is contrary to God and antagonistic to God. You should not have any part of this kind of wisdom. In fact, you should be on guard against it at all times and be very careful that you are not receiving and agreeing with wisdom that is demonic.

The ultimate wisdom is godly wisdom. It is the wisdom that comes from above. It is pure, it is holy and it is spiritually discerned. 1 Corinthians. 2:14 says,

> *But the natural man does not receive the things of the Spirit of God, for they are foolishness to him; nor can he know them, because they are spiritually discerned.*

Unfortunately, sometimes Christians can operate only by human wisdom. People like that are only really concerned about here and now, what is observable, what has been tested or studied. Their understanding is not based on the spiritual, the unseen or the miraculous and mysterious unlimited capacity of God. The source of many Christians' wisdom is not God, but instead it is often their culture, their education, or their own philosophy about life. We have to be very watchful about our wisdom and about its source, because as we will see in chapter 4, if we are not careful, we can fall into foolishness. In the next chapter, let's continue to look deeper at the wisdom and also the mystery of God.

CHAPTER

# 02

# THE WISDOM AND MYSTERY OF GOD

*However, we speak wisdom among those who are mature, yet not the wisdom of this age, nor of the rulers of this age, who are coming to nothing. But we speak the wisdom of God in a mystery, the hidden wisdom which God ordained before the ages for our glory, which none of the rulers of this age knew; for had they known, they would not have crucified the Lord of glory.*

*1 Corinthians 2:6-8*

If the demonic world knew the wisdom of God, they would not have crucified Jesus. That is very interesting because the birth of Jesus and the crucifixion of Jesus was part of a mystery, which the Bible says that God had ordained before the ages for our glory. God had packaged His plan so wisely that nobody could understand it. So when Jesus was born and lived on the earth Satan and his army did not know what God had set in motion and the Bible says if they had known the wisdom of God, they would have left Jesus alone, but God did not show them His wisdom.

Since the fall of man in the Garden of Eden, God's plan of salvation had been laid out. The challenge was how to do it legitimately. How was God going to save mankind? Adam was a human being, he sinned as a human being, he sinned as a representative of the human race, his sin brought the whole of the human race into sin, and as a result, all human beings were subject to Satan.

God started a plan to redeem man, but that plan required quite a lot because for man to be redeemed, the Savior had to be a human being. Secondly, the Savior could not have a sinful nature, the Savior had to die and shed his blood and the Savior had to defeat death and resurrect. These requirements are quite complex because if the Savior had to be a human being, then of necessity he would be a sinner, because all human beings were under sin. God had to 'sneak' in a human being who was not under Satan's control and who was not a sinner.

That process which God laid out, led to what is generally called the incarnation. The incarnation is the centre of Christmas. When we say *the incarnation* we are talking about the act of God becoming a man. The word, incarnation, is from Latin and it simply means *in the flesh* or *in body*. God physically took on flesh and manifested in a human body.

Man could not save man. God Himself had to come and save man. That was the wisdom of God in manifestation; it was the wisdom of God in redeeming us.

## The Christmas Story

There are several scriptures that tell the Christmas story. The first one we will look at in this chapter is Matthew 1:20-23. It says:

> *But while he thought about these things, behold, an angel of the Lord appeared to him in a dream saying, "Joseph, son of David, do not be afraid to take to you Mary your wife, for that which is conceived in her is of the Holy Spirit. And she will bring forth a Son, and you shall call His name JESUS, for He will save His people from their sins." So all this was done that it might be fulfilled which was spoken by the Lord through the prophet, saying: "Behold, the virgin shall be with child, and bear a Son, and they shall call His name Immanuel," which is translated, "God with us."*

The incarnation is God with us. It is not only God with us in spirit, although God is with us in spirit and He's everywhere, but in the incarnation, God is with us in the flesh. He's with us in bodily form and that is a mystery; that is the wisdom of God.

John 1:14 says,

> *And the Word became flesh and dwelt among us, and we Beheld His glory, the glory as of the only begotten of the Father, full of grace and truth.*

The Word became flesh. The Bible tells us from the start that, *in the beginning was the Word, and the Word was with God and the Word was God*. This verse is now adding that the Word became flesh. God became flesh; He incarnated Himself; He took on human form.

Philippians 2:6-8, says about Jesus:

> *Who, being in the form of God, did not consider it robbery to be equal with God, but made Himself of no reputation, taking*

*the form of a bondservant, and coming in the likeness of men. And being found in appearance as a man, He humbled Himself and became obedient to the point of death, even the death of the cross.*

The incarnation was a mystery that Satan and the demons couldn't understand. They knew God was doing something and that it was extraordinary because there were signs in the heavens and angelic visitations; they saw Gabriel moving and speaking to Mary, but they didn't really couldn't figure out God's plan. I am sure they were wondering, *what is God really up to this time? What is God about to do? What is this mystery?*

Anytime they saw the Angel of the Lord moving they tried to obstruct it. Then a Child was born and they realized He was the special One. They inspired Herod to try to kill Him, but God was smarter than that, and took the Child out of harm's way. Throughout the life of Jesus, Satan couldn't figure out what God was about to do next? The Bible says that was the wisdom of God is a mystery, which the rulers of this world did not know, because if they had known what God was working out they would have left Jesus to Himself. They didn't realize that their hatred of Him was part of the wisdom of God in action.

## The Incarnation in Christ

**In the incarnation in Christ, God became man.** Becoming a man allowed God to take on the nature of those He wanted to redeem. Prior to the incarnation, if man sinned, then man had to pay the price. God could not have done that for man as God. That would be unfair and unjust, so God became man. He united with us in the plan of salvation. In Christ, God was united with mankind and mankind was united with God. God became man and man became

God in Jesus Christ through the incarnation.

**In the incarnation in Christ, God lived with men.** God experienced the human condition. He had to live where we lived so His salvation would be complete. He felt our pain; He felt the pressures of our temptations; He felt our sense of separation; and He felt our need for redemption. You cannot redeem a people you don't fully understand and in Christ, God lived with mankind and experienced our reality.

**In the incarnation in Christ, God paid for the sins of mankind.** God had to become a man so He could pay for the sins of mankind Himself. When man sinned God concluded that the punishment was death, not just physical death, but eternal death in hell, which was a permanent separation from God. Man couldn't save himself; the one who was subject to sin couldn't deliver himself. It is like somebody who is bound at the bottom of a very, very deep pit. There's nothing to get him out. You can encourage him, but he cannot get himself out. In order to save him, someone would have to go down to where he is to get him out, but the person who goes there must have a way to climb out, otherwise there will then be two people at the bottom of the pit, rather than just one. So God had to come down to where man was, but in coming down, He had to have a plan to take man up with Him. Jesus came as the incarnate One. He was God in the flesh and He came for the sin of mankind.

There is a good analogy that helps us grasp God's mercy and grace as it was demonstrated in the incarnation in Christ. It's the story of a judge who sentenced a young man for a crime that the young man had committed. The law required that the crime be punished with a fine. So in his sentencing, the judge stated the amount of the fine, but it was a price the young man couldn't pay. The judge had sentenced and fined him according the legal process that says if you committed this crime, this is the punishment and the fine you must pay. The young man cried and pleaded, please, *I can't pay; it's too much; please have mercy, but the judge replied, according to the law, this is how much you must pay. That is the fine and if you don't pay that fine, you will go to jail.* The young man then realized he would have to go to jail because he had no money. He told the judge, *I have no parents and I have nobody to pay the fine on my behalf.* The judge maintained his position, saying *according to the law you must be fined this much,* and he exacted the full measure of the law. The law was properly applied in justice. Then after the judge had instituted the fine, he dug into his pocket and picked up the exact amount he had slapped on the man, and paid the fine himself. In that act, he became both the judge and the redeemer. This story is just like what God did for us through Christ Jesus. He became both the Judge and the Redeemer. He declared the punishment squarely according to His law, and then He paid what we could not pay. That is what the incarnation was all about – the Judge became the Redeemer.

**In the incarnation in Christ, God broke Satan's dominion over mankind.** He entered the domain of Satan in hell and destroyed his power. He died the death of all mankind, and went to hell on behalf of all of us. He overcame sin, death and hell for all of humanity, and that is why nobody should go to hell. If you go to hell, it is your fault because the price has been paid; the punishment has been borne; and the fine has been covered, but if you decide not to accept what the judge has paid for you, you will have to pay with jail time, but if you accept what He's done for you, you are made able to go free from the court. The price has been paid; Satan's dominion has been broken.

**In the incarnation in Christ, God reconciled the world to Himself.** He brought mankind back to Him. When Jesus lived on earth He was the only Son of God. John calls Him the only begotten of the Father. And so far as He was the only begotten, He was the only One who could be called the Son of God, or the Child of God. There was only one Child of God. Then one day Satan got angry, and the rulers of this world began to conspire, putting thoughts in the mind of the chief priest. They began to create jealousy in the heart of Judas; they incited a mob against Jesus and it looked like Satan was winning. First, Judas betrayed Him; then the priest arrested Him and finally Pilate crucified Him. It looked like that was the end of the story.

However, the Bible says if the rulers of this world had known the wisdom of God they would have left Jesus alone, because when that one Man died, He then had permission to descend to hell and permission to fight on behalf of mankind. It was in that process of His death and descent into hell that He destroyed every power of Satan. He stepped on the head of the serpent, He set captives free and He delivered us, once and for all, and brought eternal redemption for us.

But even that was not the end of the story. As a result of His death and resurrection, He was able to send somebody else, whom Satan had not factored in. Jesus was limited to a body, just as mankind was. He could only be at one place at one time, while he was in human form. But He said, *it is good that I go; it is good that I be killed; it is good that I be crucified because when I go, I'm going to send another One; He's not been figured out yet; His is called 'the Holy Spirit', and when the Holy Spirit comes – He's a spirit; He's not a body limited to one place – and when He comes, He will fill not only one person, but He will fill as many as believe.* So there was no longer just one Jesus; there are many 'Jesuses' because the Holy Spirit in Jesus now lives in the hearts of many who believe.

It is on this basis that we can call ourselves children of the Most High God because the Incarnate One paid the price. And the Bible says that if Satan had known that, he would have told Judas not to betray Jesus; he would have told the priest to leave Him alone; and he would have told Pilate to defend Jesus; but Satan had no clue because God was working out His divine wisdom which the Bible says was a mystery – the hidden mystery – which God had ordained before time unto our glory.

It is through the incarnation that we receive the wisdom of God and become partakers of God's wisdom. In 2 Corinthians 5:17-19 it says:

> *Therefore, if anyone is in Christ, he is a new creation; old things have passed away; behold, all things have become new. Now all things are of God, who has reconciled us to Himself through Jesus Christ, and has given us the ministry of reconciliation, that is, that God was in Christ reconciling the world to Himself, not imputing their trespasses to them, and has committed to us the word of reconciliation.*

I may not know you personally, but I know that you are the "anyone" referred to here. Whether you are male or female, this scripture is talking about you. Whether you are black or white, this Scripture is about you. It doesn't matter if you are tall or short, fat or thin, educated or not educated, rich or poor this Word applies to you, equally. You could be homeless or you can live in a mansion. It doesn't matter, because it is still talking about you. The only thing that is necessary for you to be able to claim this newness and reconciliation with God is for you to be in Christ. It does not matter who you are in yourself. What matters is who you are in Christ.

I like that phrase – God was in Christ reconciling the world to Himself. Everything that God was doing through that Man of Galilee was bringing us back to Himself. That was the wisdom of God in manifestation.

## Partakers of God's Wisdom

1 Corinthians 1:26-31 qualifies us to be partakers of God's wisdom. I like how the Apostle Paul addresses the Church in Corinth because when you read this passage you can almost feel what Paul was feeling. Remember, at this time the church is a very marginalized sub-culture in the Jewish community. They did not attract the greatest people. There were all kinds of house servants, slaves and other lowly regarded people there, and Paul looks at them and he says, *on the outside, they may not seem much, but these guys here – these slaves and servants – they are God's prized possession.* This is how he addresses them:

> *For you see your calling, brethren, that not many wise according to the flesh, not many mighty, not many noble, are called. But God has chosen the foolish things of the world to put to shame the wise, and God has chosen the weak things of the world to put to shame the things which are mighty; and the base things of the world and the things which are despised God has chosen, and the things which are not, to bring to nothing the things that are, that no flesh should glory in His presence. But of Him you are in Christ Jesus, who became for us wisdom from God – and righteousness and sanctification and redemption – that, as it is written, "He who glories, let him glory in the LORD."*

In verse 26, he didn't say that *not any* are called, but he said *not many* are. It means some mighty are called, some nobles are called, and some brilliant people are called, just not many of them. I just want to encourage some of the noble, mighty and educated to know that you can be called. You might be the only one of your peers, but it is possible. However, the people Paul is really talking to in this passage are people who have nothing and have no titles, no privilege and no status. He said to those, *look at yourselves; not many wise, not many mighty, not many noble are called, but of Him you are in Christ Jesus, who became for us wisdom from God.*

It is our being in Christ that makes us wise. It is our being in Christ that elevates us, not who we are in the flesh, but who we are in Christ. The scripture asks what shall it profit a man if he gains the whole world and loses his own soul?2 The most brilliant scientist that doesn't know Christ doesn't match you in wisdom. The most sophisticated philosopher who doesn't know Christ, cannot match you in wisdom; the richest man on this planet doesn't match in wisdom the believer who lives on the streets because what shall it profit a man if he gains the whole world and loses his own soul?

Can you imagine that there is a flood taking place and everything is being destroyed and there are rich men living in that land, but the flood is coming and the flood is going to kill them and wipe away everything, but they are just proud in their mansions and enjoying their money? At that time, the poor person in that land picks a boat and sits inn that boat and leaves the land that is being destroyed. Who in that scenario is wiser: the poor man who had the boat and left the land of destruction, or all the rich people lavishing in their fleeting luxury?

That is what the Bible means by what shall it profit you if you gain the whole world but you have no boat to escape the condemnation that is coming. Though he may not be rich, or famous, or educated, the one who has the boat is the one with the one possession that can rescue him from the land of destruction. All the rich people are left behind and are destroyed with all their things.

That boat, my friend, is not made by carpenters; that boat is Jesus and if you have Him, you are greater, you are wiser, you are smarter, you are richer than anybody else who doesn't, because He is the wisdom of God. Jesus Christ embodies the wisdom of God, whom God has given to us.

## People God Chooses

When Paul says to the Corinthian church, *you know your calling – you know who you are – you know you are not much* he described the four kinds of people as the people God chooses. In the Bible he describes them as *the things that be not*, so in a way, he described them as four kinds of *nothing*.

### *The unsophisticated.*

The first kind of person Paul described is the foolish, or those who are unsophisticated. Have you ever stopped to notice that God chooses us in our foolishness? He does not ask us to be wise before He chooses us. As a matter of fact, choosing Him is the greatest wisdom of our lives. God does not ask you to be the smartest person before He chooses you; He chooses you while you are in foolishness in order to make you wise. He chooses the foolish to put to shame those who trust in their own wisdom.

### *The weak and powerless.*

Then Paul says that God chooses the weak – those who are powerless. In the days of Paul, these were people without any social status; they didn't have titles or family names or power. They couldn't do anything by themselves or for themselves. They lived at the control of the powerful but these were the people that God chose.

## The bottom.

The third group Paul described were those who are without honour. He was talking about the base of society; those who are at the bottom of life; or what people would call the lowlifes. He tells us that God uses these kinds of people.

## The neglected and despised.

Fourth, he says God chooses the despised those who are neglected. Paul says that when God chooses these so called 'nothings', He does so to put to shame the 'somethings' of the world. That is the wisdom of God. He chose a 'nothing' David to put to shame a 'something' Goliath. He chose a 'nothing' Gideon to put to shame the armies of the Midianites. He chose a 'nothing' Esther, an orphan girl, living on the streets of Shushan as a refugee, and puts to shame an empire.

God is not looking for 'somethings;' He is looking for 'nothings.' And if you are something and you make yourself nothing before God, He will choose you and make you the wisdom of God. That is the wisdom of God. It is the greatest wisdom because His wisdom makes the wisdom of the world reveal its foolishness. You may know a few things here and there and people may call you wise but do not glory in your wisdom; it is nothing before the wisdom of God. Choose the wisdom of God. It is supreme and makes all things possible and perfect. It made a sinner condemned to eternal death with no way of escape, find a way to eternal life. One thing I have learnt never to do is to glory in my own wisdom because I have found it to be limited. However, the wisdom of God in my life has never failed me. Jesus Christ is the wisdom of God manifested in our lives and we must choose Him just as in Him, God chose us.

*CHAPTER*

# 03

# THE EXCELLENCE OF WISDOM

In this chapter, we will do a study of Proverbs chapter 8, which the Bible titles "The Excellence of Wisdom." Reading from verse 1–3 says:

*Does not wisdom cry out and understanding lift up her voice? She takes her stand on the top of the high hill, beside the way, where the paths meet. She cries out by the gates, at the entry of the city, at the entrance of the doors:*

## Where Wisdom is Found

Have you ever stopped to notice that in the Bible, wisdom is personified with the personal pronoun *she*? Wisdom is presented as a woman. The reason is to show the desirability of wisdom. It is telling us that we should seek wisdom, similar to the way that a man will look for a wife. I know many men out there are perplexed and wondering *where is she? Where will I find my wife?* Here we are given four specific locations where wisdom can be found.

## On the hilltop.

Wisdom stands on the top of the high hill. This means that wisdom is high and lifted up on top of the hill, making her visible to anyone approaching the hill. It also means that wisdom is not hidden, but exposed. And it means that above all, wisdom is elevated. It paints a picture of a stranger approaching a village and seeing a high hill as the first landmark with wisdom sitting right on top of it.

Most of the time when you hear the word 'wisdom' the first thought that comes to mind is something secretive and mystical, hidden in a remote part of the earth or in some secret place.

Biblical wisdom however differs from cultic wisdom. The wisdom of the cults is hidden in secret codes, in secret book and in secret rituals, but the wisdom of the Bible is exposed for everyone to see.

## By the wayside.

Wisdom is found on the wayside or along the way. This implies that wisdom is commonplace and anybody can have access to it and not just a selected few.

There are all kinds of secret cults that promise wisdom to their members, and to gain access to their wisdom, members are required to go through some sort of special initiation. Biblical wisdom does not require any initiation. It is by the wayside and it is common.

## Where paths meet.

Wisdom is found where the paths meet. Where the paths meet is the intersection, the crossroad or the junction.

Where the paths meet can be freely used by anybody. This analogy is more real for those who have lived in a small town or village before. Usually, there is only one intersection or junction in the whole village and every important thing happens there; that is where the village folks mingle; that is where the boys go to meet the girls; the market place is around that location and that is where people meet to discuss issues. When the people make appointments they say, "let's meet at the junction."

Wisdom is found in the place where the paths meet – at the junction of life. It is not hidden; it is accessible. If you want wisdom you are not going to find it in a secret place; it is at the place where the paths meet. Where everyone has access.

**By the gates.**

Wisdom is also found by the gates. Wisdom is inescapable. If you miss wisdom on the hill, because you were looking down and not up the hill, and you miss it by the wayside, because you were so busy you did not take note of what was happening by the wayside, and you again miss wisdom at the place where the paths meet, because you had no friend and nobody invited you to the junction, you will definitely find wisdom at the gate because you will need to go through the gate to enter your own house. You cannot miss it.

Again, from the passage, you will notice that wherever wisdom is, whether on the hill or at the gate, it is not silent. Wisdom is shouting. She has lifted up her voice and is crying, calling for attention. You have no excuse not to be wise because wisdom is so easy to access. It is exposed; it is commonplace; it is accessible and it is inescapable. Wisdom is not like that treasure that everybody wants but no one can have. The paradox of wisdom is that it is a treasure that is available to all. It is not buried deep in the earth like diamonds and gold. It does not require toil and destruction to get. It is everywhere and it is inviting. You will find her wherever you look.

The wisdom of God is available to all. Verses 4 and 5 read:

> *To you, O men, I call, and my voice is to the sons of men. O you simple ones, understand prudence, and you fools, be of an understanding heart.*

Wisdom cries out to all categories of people, but especially to the simple ones and to the fools. She calls to everybody and speaks to everybody. Each one of us has access to wisdom. No one has an excuse to be unwise. When people act unwisely, it is not because they do not have access to wisdom, it is because they have chosen to ignore the calls of wisdom.

## Wisdom's Message

If wisdom is so visible and is crying out, what is her message? When she shouts from the hilltop, what does she say? When she screams by the wayside, what's on her mind? When wisdom whispers at the junction of life, or at the entrance of the gates, what is she telling us? What is the voice and sound of wisdom and what message is she carrying?

Proverbs 8:6-9 gives us wisdom's message.

> *Listen, for I will speak of excellent things, and from the opening of my lips will come right things; for my mouth will speak truth; wickedness is an abomination to my lips. All the words of my mouth are with righteousness; nothing crooked or perverse is in them. They are all plain to him who understands, and right to those who find knowledge.*

**Wisdom calls us to excellent things.**

She calls us to what is above the ordinary; she speaks of excellent things. She challenges you to move from your current level to a higher level. Wisdom never calls you to ordinariness, mediocrity or smallness. She never calls you to the status quo and never compromises her stand. Wisdom will say, "you are doing well, but you can do better. You must improve; you must excel." When you think you are the best, wisdom will still tell you that you can be better than your best.

Take note of all the voices you hear, and discern which one is the voice of wisdom. One of the first things that will qualify whether a voice is of wisdom is when it calls you to excellent things; to excel; to think big; to be better; to overcome and to conquer your limitations.

If you are going through challenges, be it marital, moral, financial or whatever it may be, and you are counselled to accept and live with it, because such challenges are normal, instantly you have to recognize, that this is not the voice of wisdom. The voice of wisdom will encourage you to persevere, to breakthrough and to overcome your challenges.

I encourage you to conduct an audit of all the voices that speak to you and find out which voice encourages you to excellence and which one permits you to remain in your comfort zone.

Take a moment and think about the key categories of your life; family, profession, health, your spiritual life, relationships, finances and your own personal development. What situation are you currently going through? What challenge are you facing? Who is advising you? What are your internal thoughts? Are the messages concerning these areas of your life wise? Assess, and remember that wisdom will call you to excellent things.

**Wisdom speaks right things.**

The word, right, in the Hebrew language means *to be* straight and orderly. Wisdom tells us to be orderly and not haphazard. She will not call us to disorder and chaos. She instructs us to manage every aspect of our lives well relationships, resources, family, time and every other thing.

When you spend a lot of time just chatting about nothing in particular that is not wisdom. When you participate in activities that take a lot of your time, but produce little or no results that is not wisdom. Wisdom will make you straight and orderly, that is, to do the right thing.

Are you walking in wisdom? Again, take an inventory of your life in the different categories I listed above. Is your life straight and orderly or are you chaotic and haphazard? Take a good look around your bedroom. How did you leave it this morning? Will it be neat and welcoming when you return home? What about your kitchen, your living room and even your wardrobe? How do they look? Whether or not they are orderly tells you if you are being wise or not. What about your diet and eating habits? Will your current diet help you to be fit and healthy twenty or thirty years from now, or is it leading you to sickness and disease? Your honest answer will inform you if you are being wise or not. Wisdom will speak to us to keep our lives straight and orderly.

**Wisdom calls us to truth.**

The voice of wisdom is the voice of truth. Wisdom calls us to what is firm and trustworthy. Wisdom stands on solid ground. She's firmly rooted and enduring, not shallow nor deceptive.

Biblical wisdom speaks the truth. She shows us an enduring path, and cautions us to build on firm foundations instead of shortcuts and quick fixes. Wisdom does not give wrong advice on issues of life such as eating habits, losing weight, maintaining a good relationship, healthy living or prosperity. Wisdom speaks the truth – the sure, firm, and enduring foundation.

**Wisdom speaks righteousness.**

Wisdom calls us to what pleases God. Wisdom tells us to be mindful of God's will and to endeavour to please the Lord in all that we do. Biblical wisdom does not accommodate crookedness or perversion.

There are two opposite kinds of wisdom: biblical wisdom and the wisdom of this world. The wisdom of God is all of the above, but to the world, being crooked or smart in your own eyes is considered wise. Biblical wisdom calls to righteousness – pleasing God, while the wisdom of this world is crooked, perverse and fraudulent, leading to doom and destruction.

We are living in times where people do the wrong thing and try to justify it as wisdom. You work in a place where everyone is stealing company resources and someone will tell you, you have to be wise and take yours, and when you don't do it, they say you are not wise. But taking company property is not wisdom; it is stealing. You hear young ladies say you have to be wise and use what you have to get what you want. That is not wisdom; it is justifying fornication and prostitution. Is it wise to risk your life with a stranger you just met? Do you know what they carry in their bodies? Do you know what they carry spiritually? It is never wise to live in sin. Wisdom doesn't accommodate that. When you sin and attempt to justify it as wise, you are not acting in wisdom, you are perverting wisdom because wisdom speaks what is righteous.

## Wisdom's Companions

Wisdom however, does not isolate herself from others; she has six special friends who closely associate with her. In Proverbs 8:12-14, we are told who these companions are.

> *I, wisdom, dwell with prudence, and find out knowledge and discretion. The fear of the LORD is to hate evil; pride and arrogance and the evil way and the perverse mouth I hate. Counsel is mine, and sound wisdom; I am understanding, I have strength.*

The companions of wisdom are: prudence, knowledge, discretion, counsel, insight and strength.

**Prudence**, basically, is sensible behavior. To be prudent is to be able to sensibly manage whatever little you have. Prudence is careful, practical and judicious. She is not rash or hasty.

It is a disaster of life to be wasteful, especially when you have very little. Take for example, a person who earns a very low income, but when he receives his pay-cheque decides to live like a king. Or a low-income earner who is married with children, deciding to indulge in extra- marital affairs. That is not prudent.

Prudence says, "I have only one pair of trousers and a pair of shoes, but each time I step out of my room, I will be the smartest and sharpest looking person because my trousers will always be clean and neatly ironed, and my shoes will always be polished." Prudence again says, "I don't have much but I will manage what I have excellently so that when I'm faithful in little, I will be faithful in much." Prudence is sensible behavior.

**Knowledge** is learning by observation. It is not an accumulation of facts and figures in order to pass an examination.

One sad reality of many educational systems is that they are not knowledge-based, but memorization-based. Memorization is reproducing perfectly what has been committed to mind, without necessarily retaining any of the information, or synthesizing it in one's life. Nothing is observed so nothing is applied. That is how so many go through school and still end up ignorant.

Knowledge is not what is learnt in school. Knowledge is when you are able to observe the ant, observe the gecko and observe the bird and learn of their ways and apply the lessons to your life. That is why somebody who does not have any formal education can acquire knowledge. Numerous examples can be given of people who never had any formal education, but have built successful businesses and employed MBA graduates.

Knowledge is paying attention to what is happening around you. Do you notice when things change around you? Do you observe the consequences of the changes and learn lessons from them?

The ant is a very tiny creature, often times considered insignificant. But Proverbs 6:6-8 thinks otherwise. It reads:

> *Go to the ant, you sluggard! Consider her ways and be wise, which, having no captain, overseer or ruler, provides her supplies in the summer, and gathers her food in the harvest*

If you are going to be wise, you will have to be observant; you will have to pay attention; you will have to learn. That is knowledge and she is a friend of wisdom.

**Discretion** is to make good choices. Having discretion is having the freedom and power to decide what is right at any given time, but with proper consideration of our actions.

Discretion is usually misused. It is freedom to act, but freedom to act doesn't mean to be foolish. It means the freedom to be responsible. If you are given a travel allowance by your office to use at your discretion during an out-of-station official duty, and in the next town you decide to spend all the money on your lunch and groceries for your home, that is not discretion. The money is to be spent at your discretion, but your office assumes that you have wisdom too.

If I, as the General Overseer and Senior Pastor of a church have discretion to appoint other pastors, or determine how church funds are utilized, it must be exercised wisely. I must find out: is the person called, is he prepared and ready for the appointment and to serve God's people? That is how I should apply my discretion.

As a parent, particularly, the mother, you have discretion as to what to feed the family. You determine what goes on the table, but you cannot just decide that the family will eat popcorn in the morning for breakfast, ice cream at lunch and fizzy drinks for dinner. It is assumed that in addition to discretion you apply wisdom.

**Counsel** is openness to sound advice. Counsel is a friend of wisdom. Proverbs 3:7 says:

> *Do not be wise in your own eyes; Fear the LORD and depart from evil.*

None of us has all the wisdom we need for every situation in life. Good counsel comes along with wisdom. It helps us to refine our own views. Proverbs 24:6 reads:

> *For by wise counsel you will wage your own war, And in a multitude of counselors there is safety.*

Get some good counselors around you. It comes with wisdom.

**Insight** is accurate and deep understanding. Wisdom is deep; wisdom is not shallow. Wisdom investigates, wisdom asks questions and wisdom explores. Insight will help us to do that. We should not judge by sight; we judge by insight. A person of wisdom is a person of insight.

**Strength** in this context refers to the capacity to do something. It is not brute, brawn force or how big your muscles are. It is more about mental and technical capacity.

You cannot gain wisdom by building on your weaknesses. It is wise to manage your weaknesses, but you will not gain wisdom that way. For example, a bird is made to fly. That is its strength, but what if the bird decides to spend all its life learning how to swim because it admires the fish?

Wisdom calls you to find your strength and work with it. Wisdom makes us stronger and helps us to play on our greatest advantage. It is unwise to spend your life mastering your weakness, because someone who is wiser and stronger in that area will always be better. Wisdom will call you to refine your strengths and achieve excellence it.

## Wisdom's Enemies

You will notice that in the passage where wisdom named her companions, she also pointed out her enemies in Proverbs 8:13, where it says, *the fear of the LORD is to hate evil; pride and arrogance and the evil way and the perverse mouth I hate*. Wisdom's enemies are pride, arrogance, evil ways and the perverse mouth.

*WISDOM*

**Pride** is displayed when someone thinks he can do no wrong. If you are proud it means you have misled yourself to believe that you are always right. A proud person cannot handle correction or criticism. A proud person's ego is so full of itself that it cannot bear to accept fault. A person with excessive pride cannot learn, and they certainly cannot receive wisdom, because they are already wise in their own eyes.

**Arrogance** is similar to pride and is when someone has an inflated sense of themselves. They think they are more important than they actually are, or they think they are more talented, intelligent or good at something, than is really true. Arrogance is where you arrive when confidence has over stepped its boundaries. If you are arrogant it means that you have lifted up yourself so high or so full of yourself that there is no space in you for anything more. It is like an analogy I like to use, where if you put an empty cup on top of a running tap no water will enter the cup, although it is very close to the running tap. Its position on top of the tap will not allow it to receive water. If you want to fill the cup it has to go under the tap. Arrogance won't allow that. It won't humble itself to go beneath the tap and thereby it cannot receive any wisdom that is being poured out.

**Evil ways** are behaviors and deeds that are wicked, immoral and harmful. Evil ways are inspired by demonic forces and as such, cannot co-exist with wisdom borne of God. To follow evil ways means that you reject God's ways. It means you shun righteousness and embrace wickedness. Such ways are the enemies of wisdom.

**A perverse mouth** is one that speaks recklessly, deceitfully and uses vulgar language. A perverse mouth is one without restraint. A person with a perverse mouth, if they have a conscience, will feel a lot of shame and regret, because they allow their mouth to make them foolish. They lie, deceive and use filthy language that would make their mother cringe with shame. A person whose words can embarrass their mother cannot be wise. A perverse mouth breeds more trouble than peace. The Bible says that such a mouth is the enemy of wisdom.

## Wisdom's Work

Wisdom does not just cry and show us who her companions and enemies are, wisdom also tells us about her work. This can be found in Proverbs 8:22-31. It says:

> *The Lord possessed me (wisdom) at the beginning of His way, before His works of Old. I have been established from everlasting, from the beginning, before there was ever an earth. When there were no depths I was brought forth, when there were no fountains abounding with water. Before the mountains were settled, before the hills, I was brought forth; while as yet He had not made the earth or the fields, or the primal dust of the world. When He prepared the heavens, I was there, when He drew a circle on the face of the deep, when He established the clouds above, when He strengthened the fountains of the deep, when he assigned to the sea its limit, so that the waters would not transgress his command, when he marked out the foundations of the earth, then I was beside Him as a master craftsman; and I was daily His delight, rejoicing always before Him, rejoicing in His inhabited world, and my delight was with the sons of men.*

Wisdom is telling us that she has been in existence for a very long time and in verses 30 – 31, wisdom says something about her work.

Wisdom says, I've been here for a very long time. Before creation or anything started. Before the primal dust, I was here. This tells us that wisdom did not start today. Wisdom did not even start with your ancestors. Wisdom was here before the earth was formed. So when wisdom speaks, we must listen. Wisdom is smarter than our ancestors. Wisdom is smarter than our tradition. Wisdom is smarter than our culture. Wisdom is also smarter than our universities, philosophers and experts. Wisdom knows more than all of these because she was there when everything began.

**Wisdom is God's master craftsman.** This means that wisdom designs and builds things for God. When God desires something, wisdom designs and builds it. Wisdom is what produced all the things. God spoke it, God willed it, but wisdom, as God's master craftsman, designed and produced it. Whenever God wants to build something, He calls on wisdom.

Whatever God wants to build in your life, it will be designed by wisdom. When God wants to bless you, it will be orchestrated by wisdom. When God wants you to be happy, He's going to call on wisdom to deliver. When God wants you to be the head and not the tail, wisdom will design the strategy. Whatever God intends for you, He's going to call on wisdom, the master craftsman, to bring it to pass. Therefore, if you believe the promises of God, you must believe in wisdom. If you believe God has blessed you, you must believe in wisdom to make the blessing a reality because wisdom is the master craftsman. Without wisdom, you may have a great promise of God upon your life, and that promise will not become a reality because you don't have the master craftsman to translate the promise into reality.

Wisdom is the master craftsman. No wonder the Bible says in all your getting, get wisdom[3]. Whatever you want God to do in your life, you are going to need wisdom. If you want a good marriage, you need wisdom. If you want to be happy, you need wisdom. If you want to be successful, you need wisdom. If you want to overcome your enemies, you need wisdom. If you want good health, you need wisdom. The more wisdom you have, the healthier your life will be.

Whatever you need in life wisdom is the master craftsman. It is God's designer and implementer of ideas. When God wanted a universe, He called wisdom to design it. So what do you need in life? What are you believing God for in life? You need the master craftsman. You need wisdom. If you lack it, so much will remain unaccomplished in your life. So much will remain only as a promise but not become a reality because of the lack of wisdom. Wisdom is God's master craftsman.

**Wisdom is God's daily delight.** Wisdom brings happiness, delight, glory and beauty to God because wisdom manifests God's wonders to all creation. When God sees the work of wisdom He is delighted. When God sees the work of wisdom He rejoices. When God sees the work of wisdom His heart is pleased. If God sees the work of wisdom in creation and is delighted, I believe when He sees the work of wisdom in our lives, He will be delighted as well. If you really want to bring daily delight to God, then commit to walking in wisdom, because a man or woman of wisdom brings delight to God.

When you read from verses 15 – 21 of Proverbs chapter eight, wisdom talks about ruler ship, riches and righteousness. She says, "By me kings rule." It is a calamity to be in a place of leadership and not have wisdom. It is severely damaging to be positionally powerful but bereft of wisdom. When you are a father, the head of a family, and have no wisdom, you cause chaos in the life of your children. When you are a leader in any form of life, and you lack wisdom, tragedy will follow. For example, a teacher without wisdom is going to kill the confidence of his pupils. That is severely damaging, because it can affect that child into adulthood. There are teachers who insult. I remember my Class 5 teacher nearly ruined my life because of his lack of wisdom. The words you say can ruin somebody.

There are parents without wisdom who look at their own children and insult them as if they are terrorists. They fight their own children; criticize and curse them, telling them they'll amount to nothing. I always wonder about such parents, because if they are the ones who produced the child, and tell the child he will amount to nothing, then what do those parents think about themselves? There are parents, who are in leadership but run their homes with foolishness and create mayhem in their children. So you can find a family where children grow up and they are all enemies because the parents had favourites. It shows a lack of wisdom when parents do that.

Somebody's child must be last in class, so if your child doesn't do well in class, instead of disliking that child, encourage the child because the Bible says that *the last shall be the first*. It is possible for your child who is last today, to be first in their future. After all, who says that just because a child struggles with addition and subtraction, he isn't intelligent in another area? The role of a parent is as the supervisor of the destiny of that child. A parent who belittles their children, or pits one against the other, is a ruler with no wisdom.

## Wisdom's Plea

Proverbs 8 ends informing us that wisdom is pleading with us. Verses 32 – 36 says:

> *Now therefore, listen to me, my children, for blessed are those who keep my ways.*

*Hear instruction and be wise, and do not disdain it. Blessed is the man who listens to me, watching daily at my gates, waiting at the posts of my doors. For whoever finds me finds life, and obtains favour from the LORD; but he who sins against me wrongs his own soul; all those who hate me love death."*

**Listen to me.**

Wisdom is begging. What is it saying? It is saying listen to me. Be open to wisdom. Keep your ears open; keep your heart open. Hear my instruction.

**Stay with me.**

Then wisdom says keep my ways. Wisdom wants us to continue on her path and to keep walking with her. When we leave the path of wisdom, we find ourselves walking in the path of fools. Solomon is a classic case of a man who starts in wisdom but did not continue in the path of wisdom. He shows us that it is possible to start in wisdom and then depart from it, so wisdom says, when you start with me, stay on course. I beg you, stay with wisdom.

**Look for me.**

Then wisdom says watch daily at my gates. This means be alert and hungry for wisdom. This paints the picture of a hungry person who starts at the gate of a food distribution centre, waiting for the next supply of food. It reminds me of when we were children there were kids who knew how to order their steps, and they would come to your home at the right time. In fact, all of us knew how to order our steps to certain homes. We knew exactly when food would be ready and served so we could find ourselves right on time for lunch or supper because we were all watching daily at the gates. The Bible says that's how wisdom wants us to approach her – watching daily at the gates, to find out what she is saying.

**Respect me.**

The final plea wisdom makes is for us not to disdain her. Don't disrespect wisdom. This is a very important reminder because many times when we find money we disdain wisdom. When we find fame we disdain wisdom. When we find something great we disdain wisdom. When we find love, we disdain wisdom. For what would make a man in his sixties, who has lived a good life, has a decent family, and risen to a position of authority, leave all of that for a twenty-year-old girl who says she loves him, and the man believes her? He has disdained wisdom. Normally when people find what they term 'love', they disdain wisdom. That's why when people fall in love they become very foolish; wisdom just flies out of their head. When we see money, we disdain wisdom. When we find fame, we lose wisdom and wisdom is saying, *I beg you, don't disdain me because if you do, you will wrong your own soul and hurt yourself.*

Wisdom is available; it is on the mountaintop; it is by the wayside and at the junction. And if you don't find her in these three places, when you are entering your home, wisdom is standing at the door, screaming and crying and saying *I want to protect you.*

CHAPTER

## 04

# WISDOM VS. FOOLISHNESS

The Book of Proverbs is full of contrasts. The Bible usually uses contrasts to show us extremes and to help us to see differences. The Book of Proverbs highlights contrasts between actions and their consequences and contrasts amongst different types of people. One clear contrast is between the wise man and the foolish man. In Proverbs 14:15-16 it reads:

*The simple believes every word,*
*But the prudent considers well his steps.*
*A wise man fears and departs from evil,*
*But a fool rages and is self-confident.*

In the passage the Bible describes the wise man as prudent. In the Book of Proverbs the wise man is also sometimes described as the "diligent." The word 'prudent' means to be sensible. So the wise man is sensible, which means to have good judgment. That is why many institutions that manage money have a derivative of the word 'prudent' in their name. You will find insurance companies and banks either calling themselves Prudential, Prudent or Prudence. It means that they are measured, wise and have good judgment.

**A wise person is prudent.** According to the passage above, a wise person has three characteristics. The wise man:

*Examines a path before he follows.* It is a mark of wisdom to investigate a thing before you get involved in it. The prudent person considers well the steps he is about to take. People who are prudent examine a situation before they act on it. Families that are prudent take time to examine their options before they make a choice.

It is important as wise people not to jump into action until the situation is well-examined. That is why a lot of organizations invest heavily in research and development. Before a new product is launched, thorough research is done. Research is the foundation for innovation – whether creating a new product or sustaining an old one.

A wise man examines his ways; he thinks through what he does. The same process applies to a wise family, a wise business or a wise nation. There is a direct linkage between research and results. For example, it is evident that nations that invest in research achieve more and those that don't invest in research achieve less.

*Considers the consequences of his actions.* The wise person understands that actions do not stand on their own. He knows that every action will trigger a process or reaction. So with every action, he considers the consequences. Just like in most games, before any move, you consider your opponent's counter-move. Because you are wise you think of consequences. When you take an action, think of what is coming to you. You cannot take an action and hope there will be no consequences.

You cannot litter your whole city with rubbish and hope that there will be no cholera outbreak. With every step consider the consequences.

***Compares his path with God's way.*** The wise person compares his path with God's way. He sees God's way as the master plan and as a result compares his own path with God's way. He trusts the higher wisdom of God for his ways, so before he does anything, he first asks what God has said about the matter. Proverbs 19:21 says:

> *There are many plans in a man's heart, nevertheless the LORD's counsel – that will stand.*

Wisdom does not arrogate to itself final solution or does not think it is the final source of wisdom. A person of wisdom is always ready to bounce off his ideas and to seek a higher wisdom. Proverbs 11:14b says, in the multitude of counsellors, there is safety. A wise man considers his way.

A foolish person is simple. The Bible describes the fool as the simple. The word simple means naïve, childish and inexperienced. Put another way, the fool is simple minded; they are not deep in thought. It is childishness that causes a person to be simple minded. For example, a father may be playing with his child and they are having great fun. In the midst of their playing the father puts on a mask and instantly, the child gets scared. He forgets that the man in the mask is the same person he was having fun with a moment ago. The reason is because children are fooled by what they see. So even though it is his father wearing a mask, to him, the mask is the reality. That is how a simple person reacts; what he sees is his final reality. He cannot see the subsequent layers. The foolish person:

***Cannot think beyond the surface.*** When the Bible describes a fool it is a person who cannot see anything behind the scenes; he takes things on the face value. The fool is naïve and easily persuaded by what he hears. In the above passage the Bible says the simple believe every word. They are not able to critically analyze information. They believe any story they hear, believe any item they read in the newspapers, they believe anything they hear on the radio or see on the television. They believe whatever information is shared on social media and even go on to propagate such information without verification or critical examination. They are unable to independently verify truth. Simple-minded people cannot think beyond the surface and they fall victim to rumours, here say and speculation.

When you have an individual, a community or a nation like that it affects the quality of their decision making. They are easily persuaded by what they hear. The fool believes his way is always right. Because they cannot critically examine what they hear they believe that what they have heard the first time is all there is to know. When they hear one side of a story, they think they have heard everything. They don't have the patience or discipline to study alternate views.

***Has delusional confidence.*** The fool also acts with a deluded sense of confidence, but the basis of their confidence is very shallow. It is like crossing a busy road without looking out for on-coming vehicles, just hoping that you will not be hit. That, we know, is foolish, but there are people in this world who operate in that kind of confidence. If the person does happen to get hit by a car, they don't blame their wisdom, they blame the driver.

The Bible contrasts the wise man and the fool in the above ways. One researches, examines, and is careful about the steps they take, while the other hears one side, doesn't research, doesn't think deeply, but boldly acts. You then, have to ask yourself, *which of these two describe me?*

Am I the person who hears something and takes time to ask questions? If someone tells me a story or gives me some form of information, do I ask further questions? It is amazing the kinds of things people believe. People are duped all the time through Internet fraud for example, because they assumed everything on the Internet is true.

There are individuals who match the description of a fool; there are also families and communities that fit the description and, unfortunately, there are nations that predominantly act foolishly. Therefore, they get deceived day after day, month after month and year after year because they are unable to act wisely; they are foolish.

## Wisdom Builds

There are five different scriptures that convey to us that wisdom is a builder. First, let's start with 2 Chronicles 2:11-12, which reads,

> *Then Hiram King of Tyre answered in writing, which he sent to Solomon: Because the LORD loves His people, He has made you king over them. Hiram also said: Blessed be the LORD God of Israel, who made heaven and earth, for He has given King David a wise son, endowed with prudence and understanding, who will build a temple for the LORD and a royal house for himself!*

The second Scripture identifying wisdom as a builder is in Proverbs 9:1,

> *Wisdom has built her house, she has hewn out her seven pillars;*

Then in Proverbs 24:3-4, a third Scripture reveals:

> *Through wisdom a house is built, and by understanding it is established; by knowledge the rooms are filled with all precious and pleasant riches.*

Matthew 7:24 contains the fourth Scriptural evidence of wisdom as a builder. It reads,

> *Therefore whoever hears these sayings of Mine, and does them, I will liken him to a wise man who built his house on the rock:*

Finally, 1 Corinthians 3:9-10 says,

> *For we are God's fellow workers; you are God's building. According to the grace of God which was given to me, as a wise master builder I have laid the foundation, and another builds on it. But let each one take heed how he builds on it.*

We observe the following lessons about wisdom in the above passages of scripture:

In all five passages, the one thing that is very clear is that wisdom builds. That is one of the most important truths about wisdom. It is one of the most important ways to judge whether something is wise or not. Ask yourself, does it build? Is it constructive? Does it establish?

The second thing you will note from the five passages is that wisdom doesn't just build, but wisdom builds on solid rock. Jesus said this Himself in Matthew 7:24-27.

The wise man digs for deeper truths; he digs for deeper principles and does not rest until he has found an eternal truth to build on.

Wisdom's foundation is always solid and its foundation can handle heights. Your foundation determines how high you can go. And as you know, foundations are always underneath; they are usually not seen.

The foundation for our church building, Christ Temple, is about six meters deep; that is about twenty feet underground. When we were constructing we had to sink huge concrete beams called piles that were sunk down at twenty feet below, because the land we were building on was very marshy so we had to go deeper to find a solid place to build from.

Wisdom always goes deep. Unfortunately, people usually only admire what is on top. They don't appreciate or look deeper. However, if you don't have the depth, what you see on top will eventually crumble. You need foundation, and wisdom builds on solid rock. If a person tells you they are selling a medicine that cures twenty different diseases, one of which, you are suffering from, what would you do? Wisdom would ask questions. *How can one medicine cure twenty-seven different diseases? Who produced that medicine and what is their expertise? Have they been licensed to manufacture medicine? Has the medicine been laboratory tested? What were the results? What are the side effects? Who licensed the sale of such a medicine?* There are so many glaring questions that wisdom would ask. The wise person will dig deep but the simple person will just accept the information and buy the medicine at their own risk.

The third important point is that **wisdom builds with strong pillars**. Pillars refer to the support system that holds what you've built in place. Wisdom ensures that what she builds is properly structured so that it can grow and expand.

Wisdom is not haphazard; wisdom is not lazy; wisdom builds on rock; wisdom builds with strong pillars, on a strong foundation and with a strong structure.

Finally, wisdom protects what it has built. The Apostle Paul saw himself as a wise master builder and he says I have laid the foundation, let everybody take heed how they build on it. In other words, he told all of us who would come after him; don't take my foundation for granted. In wisdom Paul sought to protect what he built.

## Foolishness Destroys

While wisdom is a builder, the opposite is true of foolishness. Wisdom builds, but foolishness is not interested in building. Listen to how Proverbs describes foolishness. Proverbs 14:1 says:

> *The wise woman builds her house, But the foolish pulls it down with her hands.*

Just like wisdom, foolishness has its hallmarks and what this Scripture teaches us is that wisdom builds, but foolishness destroys. Wherever there is wisdom there is going to be something being built, something being constructed or something working its way up. However, wherever there is foolishness, there is going to be something being pulled down and something being destroyed. The contrast between wisdom and foolishness is very clear.

Because wisdom focuses on building and constructing things it has a deep respect for what other people have built. When you have labored to build your life, you tend to be respectful of what other people have done, but if you have built nothing it is very easy for you to destroy what other people have built because you have no appreciation for building or what it takes to build. Wisdom builds and foolishness pulls down.

## WISDOM VS. FOOLISHNESS

It is foolishness to build your marriage, to build your family, to build your ministry, your business or your reputation and then tear it apart. Sometimes people start with wisdom and end in foolishness. They build something and destroy it themselves. Wisdom is the part of them that built the thing, but foolishness is the part that is tore it down. So look into your life: there is a wisdom part of you and there is a foolishness part of you; there is a part of you that is always working to build, and there is another part of you that is always working to destroy what you are building.

Each one of us has both. As a matter of fact, the one who wrote this, King Solomon, had wisdom and foolishness. He built his life with wisdom and tore it apart with foolishness. Many times, people are their own worst enemies; they build and destroy at the same time. They build a reputation and tear it apart in no time. Wisdom builds, foolishness tears down.

What wisdom saves foolishness will squander. Proverbs 21:20 says,

> *There is desirable treasure, and oil in the dwelling of the wise, but a foolish man squanders it.*

A fool lives only for the present. He will squander everything that he has and never think about the future. Wisdom, on the other hand, saves for the long term, but foolishness is focused on instant gratification. It never thinks about the future when scarcity will come and there is nothing to gather.

The prodigal son wanted what the father had acquired over a lifetime and when the father gave him half of his lifetime's investment; the son squandered it in about a year. It is very easy for parents to build and for children to squander. You will find people whose father leaves them an inheritance, either of land or money or some other valuable thing that he toiled throughout the course of his life to build, and in a short time, the child squanders it all. That is foolishness. Wisdom saves, foolishness squanders. So ask yourself whether you are saving or squandering.

**Wisdom uplifts; foolishness tears down**. The words of the wise will always uplift, even when the wise is rebuking it tends to demand better performance. The words of a fool destroy. The wise parent will inspire confidence in a timid child, and the foolish parent will dampen the spirit of an enthusiastic child. One is an up-lifter, and the other is a destroyer.

A wise person will uplift their partner in marriage and not pull them down. You cannot describe your wife or your husband in derogatory terms and expect your marriage to work. You cannot call your husband unwise and expect that he will be wise. Wisdom builds; foolishness tears down. Are you tearing down your own marriage? Are you tearing down your husband? Are you tearing down your wife? Are you tearing down your work place, your children, or even yourself?

One of the things that amaze me is that sometimes you go to a workplace or a shop and the shop assistant, who is paid by the shop, is the same person telling you nasty things about the shop. And sometimes they will even tell you, *don't buy here; these people are wicked* and show you where else to buy what their shop is selling, and they forget their salary is paid from that same place. That shows you their level of wisdom. If you tear down the place that feeds you, you are the opposite of wise. Wisdom builds, foolishness tears down.

## The Foolish Builder

In the eyes of the foolish person, they are also builders; their decisions and actions build but even when foolishness tries to build, it destroys itself. Here is how the foolish build:

**The foolish person builds on the sand.** Even when foolishness tries to build, it destroys itself because foolishness builds on the sand. The foolish builder is one who is influenced by surface appearances; he doesn't take time to go beyond what the eye can see. He is very impressed by the superficial.

For example, during voting season in our part of the world, most people do not even know the difference between the major political parties beyond party colours, symbols, candidates and slogans. Regarding the party's philosophies and their stance on the critical issues affecting the citizens' lives, voters have no clue yet they cast in their vote and for some reason hope that should the storm come, it will be well and they will stand.

**The foolish builder settles on shifting grounds.** There is nothing firm in the lives of foolish people. One moment they are going in one direction, the next moment they are moving in the opposite direction. They have no conviction and no faith. If they hear today that product A is hot on the market, they abandon whatever they are doing and start trading in product A without asking questions or accounting for longevity. When they begin trading in product A and hear that product B is the hottest commodity in town, they abandon product A and go in for product B. They can hardly make up their minds about one thing. To them, life is about what is easy and convenient. If it is convenient for them to steal, lie, cheat and even betray their friends, they go ahead and do it. Their ground is always shifting.

**The foolish builder always builds for short-term success.** They only think about what they can gain now. They are very short sighted. The Bible tells us in Matthew 7:24-27 that the foolish man built his house upon the sand, the rain came up from the top; the floor came up from the bottom, the winds came from the sides and the house on the sand fell flat. You can put the blame for your failures on global challenges and so on, which are faced by all builders, yet some are still standing, while others are collapsing. It simply means the building was not rightly constructed. The foundation was wrong.

## Become a Wise Builder

If you live in a culture where people are supposed to believe everything that a person in authority says, digging deep is absent. In some cultures, children are not supposed to ask questions; what an adult tells them is considered the truth. That adult may be a foolish person, but just because he is an adult, whatever he says is accepted. When they are in school, children don't challenge the teacher, though the teacher may be wrong. The children grow through life without investigating information or truth. Before they realize it, the general society becomes one that doesn't dig deep. Everything is taken at face value and once a person in authority speaks, it is believed to be the truth. If that society wants to build wise men and women, they will have to collectively learn to dig deep.

If you want to build as a wise man, dig deep. If you want to build as a wise Christian, go beyond the words of your pastor. Study the Bible for yourself and dig deeper with Bible references to substantiate his words. Unless you learn to dig deep, your foundation can never be strong. We must cultivate the habit in our lives of investigating, examining and critically thinking through information.

For example, ask yourself, when was the last time someone gave you information and you asked questions – either of them, or even to yourself? When was the last time you heard something and decided to investigate it further? Almost everybody has a phone with access to the Internet. Do you verify information you have heard or received on that same phone? How many crosscheck the source of information, and whether it comes from a credible outlet? If you don't have the discipline of investigating truth, your foundation will be shallow, and people will deceive you.

If you are going to get married, you should also dig deep. Dig deeper beyond the clothes, the car, the apartment and the salary. Check the person's character; investigate their history, examine their principles and values, and then ask yourself questions. Don't assume that everything will be just fine.

In order to become a wise builder, you must build on enduring foundations. Don't build on popularity; build on something that is sustainable, something that is able to stand the storm and the test. In this world you will always be attacked by adversity but your foundation will keep you, either in peace or in chaos.

## The Source of Foolishness

Psalms14:1 gives us insight on what causes a person to be foolish. It says,

> *The fool has said in his heart, "there is no God." They are corrupt, they have done abominable works, there is none who does good.*

This verse tells us that those who say there is no God end up being corrupt, doing abominable works, and none of them do good. Just as the Bible tells us that the fear of the Lord is the beginning of wisdom, the root of foolishness is saying to one's self that there is no God. What then, is the meaning of that statement? It means,

**Denial of self-evident truth.**

Take note of the phrase "has said in his heart." This means he has said to himself. The fool, therefore, is the one who says to himself there is no God. The phrase doesn't say the fool believes there is no God, rather, he says to himself. In other words, the fool knows there is a God, but he convinces himself that there is no God. He knows the fact, but he willfully denies it. Underneath this verse is the whole principle of denial of self-evident truth.

What is self-evident truth? It is truth that you see; truth that is evident. For the people who deny the existence of God know there is God, but they just want to fight the truth. To them, what is self-evident is not self-evident. The fool has convinced himself that the reality is not real. So the basis of foolishness is denial of self-evident truth.

As much as the fundamental people who deny and say there is no God are atheists, there are a lot of Christians, and even pastors, who have said in their heart "there is no God," but they go to church, read the Bible, pray and worship, but have convinced themselves that there is no God, because if they believed there was God, their actions would be different. If a pastor who preaches righteousness can stand before his congregation and lie, commit adultery and cheat, and still preach boldly, then he has said in his heart, there is no God. His action is that of someone who knows reality but denies it.

It is like a person who tells his friends that he doesn't believe in the law of gravity and to prove himself, jumps from a high building and finds himself landing on the ground. When you find out his reason for jumping from the high building your reaction will shift from being sympathetic to insults, because he has said in his heart there is no gravity.

## Disregard for moral authority.

Once a person rejects a fundamental principle, they feel they are not accountable to it. Whether it is God, gravity, truth or the principle of sowing and reaping. So the fool is one who lives without rules – he thinks he makes his own rules. He has no boundaries. If he feels like doing something, he does it – with whoever and whatever. If he feels like getting drunk, he gets drunk. If he feels like sleeping and not going to work, he does just that. He doesn't think of the consequences of his actions, or that he is under obligation to receive the final end product of any process he sets in motion.

## Distortion of life's principles.

Foolishness sets in when a person takes a good principle but decides to misapply it. They take the principle of life meant for good and turn it around to do evil. They take the principle of love and turn it into lust. Some take the principle of the freedom of choice and believe that every choice is legitimate, which is not so. Many choices may be popular, but that does not make them legitimate.

In Romans 1:18-27, the Apostle Paul argues this point about people who deny self-evident truth and distort God's principles.

> *For the wrath of God is revealed from heaven against all ungodliness and unrighteousness of men, who suppress the truth in unrighteousness, because what may be known of God is manifest in them, for God has shown it to them. For since the creation of the world His invisible attributes are clearly seen, being understood by the things that are made, even His eternal power and Godhead, so that they are without excuse, because, although they knew God they did not glorify Him as God, nor were thankful, but became futile in their thoughts, and their foolish hearts were darkened. Professing to be wise,*

> *they became fools, and changed the glory of the incorruptible God into an image made like corruptible man – and birds and four- footed animals and creeping things. Therefore God also gave them up to uncleanness, in the lusts of their hearts, to dishonor their bodies among themselves, who exchanged the truth of God for the lie, and worshipped and served the creature rather than the Creator, who is blessed forever. Amen. For this reason God gave them up to vile passions. For even their women exchanged the natural use for what is against nature. Likewise also the men, leaving the natural use of the woman, burned in their lust for one another, men with men committing what is shameful, and receiving in themselves the penalty of their error which is due.*

According to the Scripture, once you deny the foundation of self-evident truth, you open yourself to acts that are shameful. If you look at the anatomy of the male and female, it is self-evident truth that they are supposed to come together. The structure does not permit male-male coming together, and vice versa for females. You don't need any logic to know this. It is self-evident truth. But when people depose God from their minds then they normalize any behavior that conforms to their own wishes. The Bible calls that shamefulness. They turn the truth of God into a lie. *The fool has said in his heart there is no God.*

There are church-going fools; there are Bible-believing fools; there are prayerful fools; there are worshipping fools; and there are pastoral fools who have all said in their hearts that there is no God because you can tell by their actions. They don't factor in God's consequences, and that is the fountainhead from which foolishness springs.

Let's look at Matthew 7:24-27 and see what Jesus Christ Himself said about the fool and the wise man.

> *Therefore whoever hears these sayings of Mine, and does them, I will liken him to a wise man who built his house on the rock: and the rain descended, the floods came, and the winds blew and beat on that house; and it did not fall, for it was founded on the rock. But everyone who hears these sayings of Mine, and does not do them, will be like a foolish man who built his house on the sand: and the rain descended, the floods came, and the winds blew and beat on that house; and it fell. And great was its fall."*

So there were foolish people in Jesus' time. This parable of Jesus is about basic foundation and not about construction material. It is about the base from which you build anything. Both the wise and foolish man used probably the same building materials. Both of them built, but what determined the sustainability of what they built was what they built on. One built on rock, the other built on sand.

In the days of Jesus there were a lot of flash floods - floods that start and end very suddenly. When it rains almost out of nowhere, there'll be a big flood that will sweep away everything in its path, and subside after about thirty minutes. This was very common so when people built houses they did so protecting against flash floods so that when the floods came their houses would remain intact. Jesus uses that to illustrate the difference between the wise and foolish man. The wise man builds to endure and establish; the foolish man builds to destroy.

CHAPTER

## 05

# TWO CASE STUDIES OF WISDOM: ELIHU AND BEZALEL

### Elihu's Wise Observations

In the Introduction, I stated the various books of wisdom in the Bible and as I said, Job is one of them. In the Book of Job you will see human beings trying to understand why things happen, and why people suffer and go through pain. When Job had his problem and lost everything, he didn't understand what was going on in his life. His friends also didn't understand what was going on in his life, so when they came they started developing arguments for why bad things had happened to him. They went on for a very long time trying to convince Job of their hypothesis, and Job likewise couldn't convince them of his position and so there was a stalemate.

In the story, there were three friends of Job who were discussing the issue, but there was a fourth person in the story as well who had not chimed in. He was a young man called Elihu. While Job and his friends were debating, he didn't speak but after some time when he had listened to the older people trying to explain what was happening, he offered up his thoughts and I want us to look at what Elihu says in Job 32:4-9 because he says some important things. Later, he took a wrong turn, but in this passage he says some important things about wisdom:

> Now because they were years older than he, Elihu had waited to speak to Job. When Elihu saw that there was no answer in the mouth of these three men, his wrath was aroused. So Elihu, the son of Barachel the Buzite, answered and said: "I am young in years, and you are very old; therefore I was afraid, and dared not declare my opinion to you." I said, "age should speak, and multitude of years should teach wisdom." But there is a spirit in man, and the breath of the Almighty gives him understanding. Great men are not always wise, nor do the aged always understand justice.

Elihu makes four important observations. The first observation that Elihu makes is that **wisdom is not based on age**. That is a very important observation. Age does not guarantee wisdom. The convention is that as a person gets older we assume that they get wiser. We assume that as people grow older in age, they learn from their lives and improve in wisdom. However, age by itself does not make one wise. It is possible to find people who are old in age, yet children in understanding. In fact, many people grow old, yet they do not change.

I told the story once where I was at a funeral, and as usual, in Ghana we dance at every occasion. People are dead and we are dancing. I was sitting there watching and I saw this old lady, probably in her eighties, and she was one of the ones dancing. I just looked at the moves of her dance, the way she was twisting and wiggling her waist and the gestures of her dance, and I thought to myself, *this is a bad girl who has not changed.* She was probably bad at sixteen and she's still bad at eighty-six. No change.

Age does not mature people. As a matter of fact, if wrong is all you know, then age can only make you more experienced in the wrong things you've always done. When you assume that because somebody is older they are wiser, you are assuming wrong, and that is what Elihu was saying. "I thought the older people knew better, but really, wisdom is not age-dependent." It would be nice if older people were wiser. It would be ideal; but the reality of life is that age does not necessarily make you wiser.

The second observation that Elihu makes is that **wisdom is not based on position**. In verse 9, he says *great men are not always wise.* Elihu realized that having a high position in life does not make you wise. Wisdom is not tied to a position or title. We Africans have high regard first, for age, and the second thing we have high regard for is titles and positions. We respect 'the big man'. Once someone with a long or puffed-up title has spoken, that is it. End of discussion. We assume the big man knows it all. Well, according to Elihu great men are not always wise.

There are people with high-ranking titles and low-ranking intelligence; high-ranking titles, and low-ranking morals; big titles, yet little wisdom, so be careful not to equate position with wisdom. This is where observation, testing and examination will serve you well. Wisdom is not title or position dependent.

If Elihu observes that wisdom is not based on title and is not based on age, what then did he observe wisdom to be based on? In his third observation, he says there is a spirit in man. What should we take this to mean? What Elihu's observation reveals is that **wisdom comes from the spirit not from the flesh**. Godly wisdom is spiritual. It comes through our spirit. He says there is a spirit in man and that is where his or her wisdom emanates.

The forth observation that Elihu makes is that **wisdom is received through inspiration**. He says, *and the breath of the Almighty gives him understanding*. The King James Version says *the inspiration of the Almighty*. Inspiration means in- breathed. Wisdom is not a wind; wisdom is a breath. A wind is strong; a breath is soft. So wisdom is usually not loud. Wisdom normally comes to us very softly. It isn't forceful; it is gentle. It doesn't shout; it comes very softly and that's why it is possible to miss wisdom because wisdom is an inspiration and it is a breath. The voice of wisdom is usually soft breath.

## Bezalel's Wisdom

I believe Elihu's observations are all correct because they agree with a Scripture I now want to shift to. The first time the Bible says that somebody has wisdom is in the Book of Exodus, and it was talking about Bezalel. Although he was the first person recorded in the Bible as having wisdom, it doesn't mean that prior to him people didn't have wisdom. Given that it is the first mention in the Bible, it is prudent for us to look at his story closely, to see what we can glean from his example as we attempt to apply wisdom in our own lives.

In Exodus 31:1-5 God spoke to Moses about the building of the tabernacle, the Ark of the Covenant and the special utensils for service in the tabernacle. What God spoke to Moses, according to the scripture, was a pattern of things in heaven. God gave the concept to Moses, however Moses had to find a way of bringing it into being. God handpicked a particular man to execute the project, and this is how the Bible describes his appointment,

> *Then the LORD spoke to Moses, saying: "See, I have called by name Bezalel the son of Uri, the son of Hur, of the tribe of Judah. And I have filled him with the Spirit of God, in wisdom, in understanding, in knowledge, and in all manner of workmanship, to design artistic works, to work in gold, in silver, in bronze, in cutting jewels for setting, in carving wood, and to work in all manner of workmanship."*

The Scripture says that God gave Bezalel wisdom, and when you look closely at the passage, you see it broken down into three similar but distinctive components. All three have specific Hebrew meaning.

First, Bezalel is described as being filled with the Spirit of God, in wisdom. Here, wisdom means **technical skill**. It means to know how to do something, and when it operates in a person, it gives the person the ability to execute. Everyone who excels in a field has wisdom in that field. It is more than just having talent; it is a highly developed competency, and that's what the word 'wisdom' here means – to be technically skilled.

It is always important to understand context the first time the Bible uses words. To the Greeks, wisdom was philosophical. They thought of wisdom in terms of knowledge and theory. But for the Hebrews, which is the context that applies here, wisdom was very technical and very practical. So wisdom in that passage means technical skill, not theoretical insight.

The second thing God gave to Bezalel was understanding. Understanding in this context is **the capacity to think**. It deals with the ability to reach reasonable conclusions, the capacity to think logically, strategically and critically. So he had technical skill and the capacity to think. That is very important because every profession in the world is a thinking profession. Every job in the world is a thinking job. Even professions that appear only to be physical are in reality, thinking professions. For example, if you take professions like boxing, you may say it is only about having muscles and physical strength, but boxing is a thinking sport. Mohammed Ali told us that, and we learn that you can have the biggest muscles and still never win a match and somebody who is skinny, but thinks strategically, can outsmart you.

So professions that look only physical like athletics, music or acting are not just about physical manoeuvres; it is about thinking – the capacity to think and understand. God gives us understanding in our areas of expertise.

The third attribute Bezalel was given was knowledge. The word knowledge means **to be a master in something**; to be on top of the issue or to know something fully. In the context in which it is used here, Bezalel was called to construct the tabernacle, and not only to construct the tabernacle, but also to build the Ark of the Covenant and to develop all the other tools that would be used there. It was going to require competent skill, the capacity to think, and he had to be on top of his job.

## Wisdom and Workmanship: In Theory and in Practice

From the account of Bezalel, we learn that wisdom in the Hebrew world has these three components: technical skill, capacity to think and the ability to stay on top of what you are doing. I want us to pay careful attention to verse 3. God says, *I've filled him with the Spirit of God, in wisdom, in understanding, in knowledge,* and then He goes on to say, *in all manner of workmanship*. This combination of ideas tells us that wisdom is related to workmanship. It is not just related to abstract philosophies and theories; it is related to workmanship. Workmanship has to do with your trade, your occupation and your business.

In every area of workmanship we need wisdom. In every area of trade, in every profession, and in any business, we need wisdom in workmanship. My workmanship is what I'm doing; that's my job, my occupation, that's my vocation; that's my calling; I'm a pastor. I have to preach, and in doing this as my workmanship, I need technical skill, capacity to think and I need to stay on top of my job. If my job were carpentry, I would still need technical skill, capacity to think and I'd need to stay on top of it. In whatever work we do, we need technical skill, capacity to think and to stay on top of our job.

**The Ability to Design a Plan**

God says two things about Bezalel's workmanship. He says that Bezalel will have the ability to design. That means to work out a plan. The wisdom that God gave Bezalel was to help him to design something; to plan out something and to work out a plan. God spoke His intention to Moses. Moses made the intentions known to Bezalel, but Bezalel had to find out how to implement it and it required wisdom. That's a very important part of wisdom.

On November 12, 2014, we listened as scientists explained how they were able to land a spacecraft, the Rosetta Philae lander, on a comet after a ten-year trip. It started its movement ten years prior and was able to land on a moving comet in space. In the process, the spacecraft travelled a total distance of over 6.4 billion meters and the comet it landed on was just four kilometers wide, and was travelling at a speed of 135,000 kilometers per hour.[4] So something that was launched from the earth ten year earlier, travels over six billion miles, lands on a comet that is just four kilometers in diameter and the thing itself was travelling 135,000 kilometers per hour. If you look at it, you will say it is impossible, but it has been done. That's wisdom; that's technical competence.

Wisdom helps us to design solutions. If people can land an object ten years away, six billion kilometers afar, that is running at that speed, and safely land it, I think we should be able to design solutions for electricity supply in Ghana. Don't you think so? We should be able to. This is not rocket science.

But wisdom is the ability to design a plan, and Bezalel was going to design a plan to translate a heavenly idea into a physical reality. It takes wisdom to take something that nobody has seen or touched, and make it a reality. Wisdom is a designer, it works out a plan and not only does wisdom design, it says that Bezalel will design and work. He would cause things to be; he would make things, he will manufacture.

**The Ability to Make Things Work**

For the Jews, when God speaks about wisdom, they are not thinking about just abstract ideas; they are thinking about taking abstract thought and making it practical; practical application of knowledge. It is possible to have solutions on paper, which do not work on the ground. The relevant question is not *does he have a degree? Does he have a Ph.D.? Have experts considered it?* The key question is *does it work?*

Wisdom produces things that work. I think many of us are overwhelmed by titles. We say, well, the guy has a Ph.D. Good! He went to Harvard. Good! He's with the U.N. Good! He works for the IMF. Great! That is all nice, and wisdom patiently waits and listens to the nice titles and affiliations, then it asks, *does whatever he is trying to do work?* Wisdom is not an abstract theory; wisdom is about designing practical solutions that work.

So let me make these three statements about wisdom:

- Wisdom always has a plan. If you are a man of wisdom, you must always have a plan.

- Wisdom designs solutions. Wisdom isn't the one analyzing or explaining a problem; wisdom is the one solving it.

- Wisdom produces results. Wisdom doesn't just about talk and theorize about an issue; wisdom resolves the issue.

There are people who are fascinated and satisfied with talking about things, but to the people God spoke to in the Bible, He wasn't just talking about things; discussing problems; he's talking about finding real solutions; to design and to work.

When you read the story about Bezalel, you see that he was able to work intricately with all kinds of tools and all kinds of objects such as fabric, gold, brass, wood, and stone. He designed clothes; he designed instruments; he designed the Ark of the Covenant so that God could manifest in it. And the Bible says that everything he did on earth was a pattern of something in heaven. He was interpreting heavenly ideas here on earth. That's what wisdom is supposed to do – interpret God's solutions in real practical terms.

When Bezalel had finished all his work, Moses looked at what he had done and said, "You've created exactly what God spoke to me about," and right after that the Bible said the glory of the Lord fell upon it. Wisdom will manifest the glory of God. Wisdom will bring God on the scene; wisdom will allow God to interact with man; wisdom will allow the power of God to reach out to people.

If we want to minister to people, after we have prayed, we must have wisdom to allow God to minister to people through us. For example, if today we pray for widows, for single people, for orphans, and for the poor that God will meet them, our work is not done there. After we've prayed we need to look for wisdom to find out how to facilitate God's interaction with people. Like Bezalel, God will grant us the plan. God will grant us solutions and programmes, He will give us the wisdom to design responses that meets the need. That is how wisdom operates. It takes a heavenly idea and translates it into an earthly programme that can be implemented and accessed by men and women.

Wisdom always has a plan. Wisdom will design a solution and wisdom will produce results. If you find a problem that is not being solved, it is reflective of a lack of wisdom. If you find persistent problems in your life, in your marriage, in your nation, in your company, it is symptomatic of a lack of wisdom. The lack of wisdom makes problems persist for a long time.

Let me just say here that the problems we have in much of Africa are very rudimentary and very fundamental. We are not even thinking of going to the moon, we are not thinking of going to Mars; we are not thinking of trying to build the tallest building in Africa or in the world. We are not thinking of building a skyscraper that has five hundred floors; we are just thinking of people not urinating in public, managing rubbish, keeping lights on, and water flowing. If we cannot deal with these low-level issues, then when will we ever put a man on the moon? Wisdom designs solutions. In chapter 31, verses 1-3. It reads,

> *Then the LORD spoke to Moses, saying: "See, I have called by name Bezalel the son of Uri, the son of Hur, of the tribe of Judah. And I have filled him with the Spirit of God, in wisdom, in Understanding, in knowledge, and in all manner of Workmanship."*

So Bezalel's wisdom is based on the inspiration of the Almighty. Wisdom comes from God. So that's why you can find somebody who is young in age but whose spirit is in tune with God, and therefore wisdom will flow through him. Conversely, you can find somebody who is older whose spirit is not in touch with God and you won't find a trace of wisdom in their words or actions.

CHAPTER

# 06

# SOLOMON'S WISDOM

We've looked at Bezalel, the first man with wisdom and we've said that his wisdom was practical and focused on planning, design, solutions and results. Now, we are going to look at Solomon, the man who is most associated with wisdom. Why is Solomon the figure most associated with wisdom throughout history? How was his wisdom demonstrated?

To further examine the nature of Solomon's wisdom, let's look at two examples on display in the Bible, first in the visit by the queen of Sheba, and then at Solomon's judgment in the story of the two harlots.

## Solomon's Peer Evaluation

Beginning with the story of the queen of Sheba's visit, this story is instructive for us because it was in essence, a visit of evaluation. The queen of Sheba had heard about the wisdom of Solomon, so she wanted to evaluate it herself. Though his subordinates considered Solomon wise, the queen's visit subjected him to higher scrutiny. When a person's juniors say they are wise, that is nice, but they could be saying it out of fear, knowing the power you have over them. You cannot always believe the evaluation of your subordinates, because they owe their existence to you, and their standard may not be as high as a person higher or equal in rank to you.

The queen of Sheba was coming to do a peer evaluation. She was also a monarch; she ruled over people and didn't owe her throne to Solomon. She was a queen, and therefore equivalent to Solomon, so her evaluation would come from first-hand knowledge of the job Solomon has to do, and would therefore have a higher standard of determining whether he was as wise as people said he was.

Your best evaluation for wisdom is not from people who depend on you, but people who are both independent and hold an equal or higher position as you. They can more accurately evaluate your wisdom. So this is a high evaluation of wisdom and I want us to look at how this monarch, this very important visitor, reviewed Solomon.

The first evaluation the queen of Sheba put Solomon through was a verbal evaluation and the second was a practical evaluation. The verbal test is found in 1 Kings 10:1-3, and it says:

> *Now when the queen of Sheba heard of the fame of Solomon concerning the name of the LORD, she came to test him with hard questions. She came to Jerusalem with a very great retinue, with camels that bore spices, very much gold, and Precious stones; and when she came to Solomon, she spoke with him about all that was in her heart. So Solomon answered all her questions; there was nothing so difficult for the king that he could not explain it to her.*

This was the theoretical test. It was the verbal evaluation of whether he had the right answers. The queen arrived in a very impressive way; she came with a convoy and she came and says "I've heard you are wise, now let's prove it." There are three things I want us to look at here. They are the test Solomon faced, his attitude and the outcome.

## The Test of Solomon's Wisdom

The Bible says the queen of Sheba tested King Solomon with hard, perplexing questions. The phrase translated for 'hard questions' makes reference to riddles, enigmas, puzzles, conundrums and questions that are difficult to answer. It is likely that there were problems facing the queen of Sheba in her own kingdom. So I imagine she came with some of the hard questions that she was grappling with herself. That sounds like a fruitful presidential visit, don't you think? She essentially said to Solomon, "Since everyone says you are such a wise ruler, tell me, *How do you structure the economy? How do you keep workers happy and prevent them from going on strike? How do you maintain uninterrupted electricity supply? How do you solve homelessness?* How would you tackle these problems? What are the answers to these questions?"

One principle we can glean from this is that **wisdom will always be tested.** Your wisdom will be challenged. The wisdom of a family will be tested; the wisdom of a business will be tested; the wisdom of a nation will be tested. The theory may appear right, but you will only be sure when it is put it to the test. It is very easy to say an idea will work when it is in your head. It is easy to believe it will work when you put it in a neatly written business plan or see it in a government policy written by an expert consultant. The question that must be asked is, what if circumstances vary or deviate what you have in the written plan? Will it still work?

The queen of Sheba bypassed the theory of Solomon's wisdom and put it to a concrete test. There'll be a test of your wisdom. Poverty will test your wisdom; marriage will test your wisdom. Every person who has been married for even a short while will tell you love will be tested. It is very easy to say you are in love and that this is the man or woman you love with all your heart. That's nice, but unfortunately it is not what matters most. What really matters is how you respond when your love is tested, because it will be. Whatever wisdom you apply in life will be tested. That is the first thing we can learn from the story.

## Solomon's Attitude to the Test

The second thing we can draw wisdom from is Solomon's attitude to the test. The Bible says in verse 3 that there was nothing so difficult for the king that he could not explain to her. Solomon's attitude was "nothing is too difficult." Solomon had an attitude that said "no problem; I can think through this; I can figure out a plan; I have the capacity and skill to solve problems." So no matter how perplexing the problem was, Solomon approached it with confidence that he could find the solution.

Wisdom does not panic before problems or run helter-skelter. **Wisdom is always calm in the face of tests.** It does not act hastily, because wisdom approaches a problem and says, 'nothing is too hard; I can solve it.' That's the mark of wisdom. When you approach situations and say, 'I can solve it; I may not know the solution right now, but I can figure it out; I haven't thought enough about it, but I can solve it, because I have the technical skill, the capacity to think and I will stay on top of this problem. I can solve it.' If you are a man of wisdom, that's how you speak. If you have a marriage problem, you say, *we can solve it*. If you have a financial problem, you say *I can construct a plan*. You don't go around in a frenzy complaining to everybody saying, 'do you know what my wife has done? Do you know what my husband did? Wisdom says, 'nothing is too difficult; we can solve this issue.'

I don't know what problem you are dealing with, but the first step to victory over it is to assume the attitude and perspective that you can solve it. So, I can imagine, the queen of Sheba asks Solomon a question, and before he even thinks of the answer he say, 'no problem, I can solve that.' That attitude by itself gives you confidence to master the problem. People of wisdom don't panic when problems appear. They put their thinking hats on.

## The Result of Solomon's Test

Now, let's look at the result in our examination of Solomon's wisdom, because **wisdom will always produce results**. The queen of Sheba left with all her questions answered. Wisdom provides answers. She had come to test Solomon's wisdom with hard questions and Solomon had passed the verbal test. Now, it is very possible to pass the verbal test the theory – and not pass the practical test. It's like what happened when we were studying music in Secondary School. We knew the treble clef, the base clef, we knew the musical notes – f, a, c, and e; and there was 'every good boy deserves favour always'. We were told this is 'middle C', but we had never touched the piano and didn't know how it sounded. So in theory, we could pass, but if you put a piano before us, we would fail. There are people who have endless theoretical answers, there are numerous armchair coaches and backseat drivers, but when you put them on the field or behind the wheel, nothing works.

Wisdom does not just work in theory, it works in practice too. We saw it in Bezalel. He had the theory, and he had the practice. Yes, he could design, but his outcome also worked. Solomon had passed the theoretical test - the verbal test. Now, comes the second test. The queen of Sheba then evaluated Solomon's wisdom from a practical point of view. She tested how his wisdom was applied. That example is found in 1 Kings 10:4-8,

> *And when the queen of Sheba had seen all the wisdom of Solomon, the house that he had built, the food on his table, the seating of his servants, the service of his waiters and their apparel, his cupbearers, and his entryway by which he went up to the house of the LORD, there was no more spirit in her. Then she said to the king: "It was a true report which I heard in my own land about your words and your wisdom. However I did not believe the words until I came and saw with my own eyes; and indeed the half was not told me. Your wisdom and prosperity exceed the fame of which I heard. Happy are your men and happy are these your servants, who stand continually before you and hear your wisdom!"*

Remember, earlier she said *I have heard.* Now she says *I have seen.* A person can hear information, but proof is not heard. Proof must be seen. Likewise, wisdom will not only be heard, but to really prove it is indeed wisdom, it will be seen. I can see the parameters of your wisdom by looking at your life, and you can see the parameters of my wisdom by looking carefully at mine. How did she see all the wisdom?

In verse 6, she makes a clarification when she says; *it was a true report, which I heard in my own land about your words and your wisdom.* Note how she makes a distinction between Solomon's words and his wisdom. Why did she speak separately of them? Because your words are not your wisdom. The audible isn't where your wisdom is shown. It is shown by the visible. Your wisdom really is what you do.

# 7 Demonstrations of Solomon's Wisdom

The queen of Sheba heard Solomon's words but she saw his wisdom. What did she observe and count as wisdom? In the passage she noted seven things.

**1. Structure**. The first thing the queen noticed was the house he had built. Surely, the queen of Sheba also had a house, and had seen various houses, but she found something remarkable about the house Solomon had built. The house represents structure. The first thing you notice about a person's wisdom is the structures he has built; the structure of his life; the structure of his habits; the structure of Solomon's home, which was called the Forest of Lebanon.

Usually, the first thing people will use to assess you is what you have built. What have you built? If you interview for a job, they'd want to look at what you have built to determine what you can build. They ask *what have you done?* We call it your resume or your CV, but it essentially tells what you have built. Normally, we say that during interviews people are looking for experience, and I'm young and don't have experience and I'm now starting to work. No, it is not about how long you've worked, it is about what have you built. Because if someone is going to hire you they want to know what you have built so they can determine whether you can build what they need you to build in the role they are interviewing you for.

What structures have you built; what are your achievements? The queen of Sheba could tell that a lot had gone into what Solomon had built. It was a durable structure; it was a beautiful structure. These details reveal the builder's wisdom. Wisdom is seen first and foremost by what and how a person has built. Jesus said that the wise man built his house on the rock. Paul said that as a wise master builder, he laid the foundation for the Church. Wisdom builds enduring, functional and graceful structures. So we must not be confused. Money does not build; it only buys. Time does not build; it only passes. It is wisdom that builds.

The structure of your life, your family, and your relationships are all the things you are building, and anyone paying attention can evaluate you, and you can evaluate them based on what they have built. Some good questions to ask yourself to assess your wisdom are *how have I built my marriage? How have I built my children? How have I built my relationships? How have I built my business or my profession?* You evaluate by structure.

**2. Supply.** The second thing the queen of Sheba saw about Solomon was his supply: the food on his table. There was something about his food that intrigued the queen. Was she hungry? No. Didn't she have food to eat? Certainly. Was that the first time she had seen food? No. It wasn't just the availability of food; it was the provision of food. Solomon kept a constant supply of food in his court. His table was never lacking; there was abundance for everyone's need.

Wisdom is seen in the provision people make for themselves. Is there food on their table? Are they able to provide for themselves, their family or their employees? Are they able to supply the needs they are responsible for? Because if a person cannot put food on their table, there may be a problem with their wisdom. Is there a constant supply of resources at your table? Wisdom does not oscillate between supply and scarcity. Wisdom builds on a system of reliable supply. The queen of Sheba realized that at any given time there was something on Solomon's table.

There are people with money who cannot maintain a steady supply. One moment they have an overflow, and in the next moment, they are begging for help. That is not wisdom. Wisdom builds and maintains constant supply. That is the second thing the queen saw; that Solomon had a constant supply. There was no shortage.

**3. Staging.** The third manifestation she saw was the staging. She describes it as the sitting of his servants. To stage something means to present something meticulous and immaculate. When we say that somebody is staging something, it means that it has been thought about, it has been choreographed and it has been well displayed. It is a production.

So when the queen went into Solomon's court she saw that people were not just sitting haphazardly. Everything had been thoughtfully placed, scheduled and rehearsed like a stage production. Wisdom does not leave things to chance. People sat in their appointed places; and people followed the schedule. When you went into Solomon's court, you knew you couldn't just walk in and sit anywhere. There was staging, planning, scheduling, and order.

Do people know they cannot just flow in and out of your life? If your life is not well-staged, people will feel they can just pass by anytime without an appointment and distract you. When people think they can interrupt you at any time and make you run on their schedule, your life is not well staged; things are not properly seated. The queen of Sheba observed the staging of Solomon's court as evidence of his wisdom. From the highest rank to the lowest rank, everybody was properly seated and they all knew and executed their role. She didn't find a slave sitting in the king's chair, and the king sitting in a slave's chair.

Sometimes in certain places, you cannot tell who is in what chair, because the chairs are not well staged; there is no proper order.

There are environments where people talk who should not be talking; people act who should not be taking certain actions. People issue statements, which they are not authorized to issue. You wonder; whose seat are they sitting in? There is no proper production. People don't expect to come to our church and find everybody talking anyhow. You won't find the person who is supposed to give announcements turning the announcement into prayer topics, or the person who is supposed to lead prayer preaching with the prayer. We have built wisdom in our staging. Everyone knows their role and they execute it as planned, and that is because one of the things we try to do in our church is to stage what we do. We take it as a proper production. Because wisdom is in the staging; in the production; in the thinking that goes behind what you do. The queen of Sheba noticed that kind of thoughtfulness and staging in Solomon's court.

**4. Service.** The fourth thing the queen of Sheba observed was the services offered in Solomon's court. She saw prompt responses of the servants. When a diner needed service, the servants were there to meet the need. Service was responsive, beautiful to watch, prompt. If something spilled on the floor, they cleaned it up instantly. When somebody is causing a commotion, they reposition the person quickly. You don't have a situation where people are disturbing, and think it is all right because that is how people are. No. You don't leave people to be people; people must be managed. And the service must manage things.

It's like you come to church and say, *we just move as we are led; we just flow in the spirit.* If I'm preaching and you are flowing in the spirit, you will be serviced. We will service you out because when the singers are singing, the attention is on them. When I am preaching, the attention is on me. When they are singing I don't come up and start preaching. No. There is proper production.

So when the queen of Sheba saw it, she said 'wow'. No food is spilled on the floor; no wine is spilled on the floor; everything is taken care of because the servants are on top of what is happening.

**5. Security**. The fifth thing the queen of Sheba noticed was the security in Solomon's house. If you saw a cupbearer in the days of old, it looked like they were just giving wine to the king, but the cupbearer keeps his eye out for every detail in the place because the cupbearer works closest to the king. They are responsible for the king's security. On the surface they just seem to be serving wine, but in reality they are bodyguards protecting the king.

The cupbearers were there also to make sure the king is not poisoned. Because in those days people were assassinated easily and the number one way to assassinate someone was to poison their food. The cupbearer was making sure no poison got to the king. She could tell that before anybody could get to this king, he had to cross this cupbearer. The king would never accept a cup from anyone except the cupbearer.

You cannot just go to the king and say you are from the village and you are just bringing him a goat to eat, or some palm wine to drink. The cupbearer will say 'yes, you love the king, yes, you want to give him palm wine, yes, you want to serve him, but you go through me first so I can determine what is in the goat and in the palm wine. The cupbearer knows that the king is so important that if he falls there is danger for the whole kingdom. The cupbearer can fall and a new cupbearer will come into place, but if the king is poisoned, everyone is in trouble because instability will threaten the whole kingdom. So the cupbearers made sure that they screened what reached King Solomon.

**6. Style**. The sixth thing the queen of Sheba saw was style. Your wisdom is seen in your style. The Bible describes the apparel of his servants. The queen of Sheba noticed the sense of style and elegance in Solomon's court. Everyone who was on duty was dressed for their role.

Wisdom is manifest in your sense of style. The way you dress influences the way people address you. What does your style say about your wisdom? Is your style classic, is it traditional, contemporary, casual or formal? Is it African; is it European? What is your style?

Wisdom will show consistency in what you are trying to do. What is the style of your furniture at home? Is it antique, modern, Chinese, minimalist, or just cluttered? What message does your home communicate? Your style is an extension of your wisdom. I try to dress according to a deliberate intentional style. I don't just wear clothes because they are nice; I wear them because there is a consistent statement I am putting forward about my personality and my worldview.

Likewise, people will notice that Christ Temple is decorated according to a consistent style and method. It says we are proudly African, we are orderly, we are clean, we are neat, we appreciate art, creativity and nice things. As you build your house, be intentional about your style. Not to follow the latest trends, but to communicate what your household is all about. If your sitting room is set up in Indian decor, your bedroom is like China, your children's bedrooms are like Germany, then people will be confused about the statement of your style. Will it say that you were just going to the market and you saw this thing so you brought it home? If the queen of Sheba came to your home, she'll leave and say, *I've heard, but what I've seen, no, no, no*. Be deliberate in your style, and give proof of your wisdom.

**7. Spirituality.** Finally, the seventh and most important thing that the queen of Sheba saw was the spirit of Solomon's court. The Bible said she looked at the entryway to the House of the Lord. Actually, that phrase about the entryway in the real Hebrew is a reference to the sacrifices he made to go into God's presence.

I'm sure the queen of Sheba was looking at everything happening, and asking herself *what is Solomon's secret? How is he so together? How does everything look so orderly and work so smoothly? What is the secret?*

Then she saw Solomon rise, and she saw Solomon going into the House of the Lord, and she saw the reverence by which he approached the House of the Lord, she saw the sacrifice, and she saw the order and she saw the dedication to God, then she understood. I can imagine her recognition of Solomon's secret and saying to herself, *the fear of the Lord is the beginning of wisdom*. The Bible says when she saw that *there was no more spirit in her*. She said, *now I know, this is why this guy is so wise*. This is the secret. He knows how to approach God, how to honour that which is sacred; things that are important; his sense of reverence; that is what is flowing down through everything he touches. Because he has reverence for God, he organizes his life according to the same meticulous, systematic reverence for God. That's why his servants are ordered because that's how he approaches God. That is why his servants are well dressed, because that's how it is in the temple; the priests are well dressed; everything is orderly in the temple, and he has taken the order of the temple and made it his lifestyle.

And when the queen of Sheba realized that, there was no more spirit in her. The fear of the Lord, not running away from God, but the respect for God is the beginning of wisdom.

If you want to be wise you should not settle for just being familiar with God and take God for granted. There has to be a certain reverence and a certain respect for things that are sacred, and when you learn to do that in the presence of God, you will learn to be sacred in your home, you will be sacred in your office; sacred wherever you operate because you will insist on being well arranged as it was in the house of God. The queen of Sheba, after all of that says, *I heard it, but what I saw today in that court of yours, when I saw all these seven things, is not to be compared to what Newsweek said and what Time magazine said and what Forbes magazine said. It's beyond what I saw on YouTube. This is mind- blowing.* And then she says *I hope those who are around you appreciate it. Happy are your servants who stand daily and see this.*

## Solomon and the Two Mothers

In chapter 4, we learned that wisdom builds, but foolishness tears down. A good illustration of this is found in one of the most celebrated stories of wisdom associated with King Solomon. It is the story of the two harlots in 1 Kings 3:16-28 and it reads:

> *Now two women who were harlots came to the kings, and stood before him. And one woman said, "O my lord, this woman and I dwell in the same house; and I gave birth while she was in the house. Then it happened, the third day after I had given birth, that this woman also gave birth. And we were together; no one was with us in the house, except the two of us in the house. And this woman's son died in the night, because she lay on him. So she arose in the middle of the night and took my son from my side, while your maidservant slept, and laid him in her bosom, and laid her dead child in my bosom. And when I rose in the morning to nurse my son, there he was, dead. But when I had examined him in the morning, indeed, he was not my son whom I had borne." Then the other woman said, "No!*

*But the living one is my son, and the dead one is your son." Thus they spoke before the king. And the king said, "The one says, 'This is my son, who lives, and your son is the dead one;' and the other says, 'No! But your son is the dead one, and my son is the living one.'" Then the king said "Bring me a sword." So they brought a sword before the king. And the king said, "Divide the living child in two, and give half to one, and half to the other." Then the woman whose son was living spoke to the king, for she yearned with compassion for her son; and she said, "O my lord, give her the living child, and by no means kill him!" But the other said, "Let him be neither mine nor yours, but divide him." So the king answered and said, "Give the first Woman the living child, and by no means kill Him; she is his mother." And all Israel heard of the judgement which the King had rendered; and they feared the king, for they saw that the wisdom of God was in him to administer justice.*

What do we learn from this story?

First, there are two women, and the Bible describes both as women and as harlots. For those who don't know, a harlot is a prostitute, so it is not as if one had a better moral life than the other. They are both harlots and the fact that the Scripture does not mention their husbands gives the indication that they are unmarried, yet with children.

It was a situation with their children that brought them to King Solomon. One of the women was wise, or at least I describe her as a wise woman in the context of what happens, and the other we'll describe here for the purpose of our illustration, as foolish. Although both were harlots, one was wise and the other was foolish. In every profession you will find the wise and the foolish, but that is not an encouragement to be a harlot; it is to let you know that foolishness can be found everywhere, and wisdom can be found everywhere. At every level of life, from the lowest to the highest, you can find foolishness and you can find wisdom.

## The Foolish Mother

Let's first look at the foolish mother. Before the case ever came before Solomon, each woman had given birth to a child, and what we learn right away about one of the mother's is that **she was reckless**. She slept on her baby and suffocated him. She was not aware of her baby's presence when she slept. She slept deeply and forgot that there was a fragile life lying by her.

One of the things you master as you grow is to be aware of what is beside you, even as you sleep. That's why we don't fall off our beds when we sleep. No matter how narrow your bed is, somehow, your mind registers the limits of your movement in your sleep, and you don't fall off your bed, because sub-consciously you are aware there is an edge to the bed you are sleeping on.

Now, I'm not a woman and I've never given birth to a child, but I've had children and have been on the same bed with children, and from my experience, the moment a small baby lies by your side, sub-consciously, the same thing that causes you not to roll off the bed registers in your mind, and no matter how much you toss in your bed, you are conscious that there is a fragile life beside you.

Once in a while, people sleep and forget, and the moment you touch the baby or get close to the edge, instinctively, you register yourself and come back. This woman slept on her child and it wasn't just a momentary sleep, the Bible says she laid on her child, which means she was there for a very long time and never had the consciousness that she was smothering him. Perhaps the child screamed, or twigged, or struggled but she never felt it. There are people who never feel it when they are destroying someone's life. They don't even feel it. It highlights their total recklessness.

The second thing about this woman was that she was deceitful. Rather than admitting what she had done, she tried to exchange her dead baby. She attempted to exchange what she had destroyed for what another woman had preserved. Instead of accepting responsibility and mourning over her dead child, she sought to shift responsibility. There are people who are reckless, and to cover up their recklessness, they are deceitful. When they destroy, they turn around and want to steal what has been preserved. They destroy their own marriage and want to steal somebody else's spouse. They destroy their own peace by whatever means, then they steal somebody else's peace. They destroy their own joy, so they try to steal yours. This woman was not only reckless, but she was also deceptive. She tried to shift what she had killed onto another woman, and tried to take what that mother had spent time to preserve.

The third thing about this woman, not only was she reckless and deceitful, but she was secretive. The Bible says that she acted in the night. She used the cover of darkness to commit her crime. She felt she could hide when nobody was watching. She acted in darkness and hoped that when it came to light she would bully her way through and gain what she had not toiled for. And there are people like that; reckless, deceitful, scheming and secretive; destroying what they have and trying to steal what other people have. Killing what they have, and stealing what others have preserved. That is the foolish woman.

## The Wise Mother

Then there is the second woman, whom I call the wise mother. The first thing the Bible says about her was that she laid by the side of her baby. **She was responsible**. She was a companion to her baby. She was aware of the baby she had given birth to. She knew she was responsible for the safety of what she had produced. And when she slept her sub-conscious mind was aware of where the baby lay. She knew "I've given birth to something; and I have to protect it. Even when I'm asleep, I have to be aware; I have to protect what I have." She was very responsible. She gave birth to a child and she protected it. She laid by the side of the baby.

The second thing you will note about this woman was that **she was diligent**. In verse 21, it says *and when I arose in the morning to nurse my son there he was, dead, but when I had examined him in the morning, indeed, he was not my son, whom I had borne*. Two things stand out here: That she rose in the morning. The word morning means dawn. She rose at dawn to feed her child. That is a very responsible thing to do, but that is when she realized the child was dead. Then she said, 'I cannot make a decision in the dark, I'm going to wait for the morning light' and when the morning light came she examined her child.

She has a keen sense of awareness, keen sense of recognition, a high sense of responsibility and she could tell what was hers and what was not. Some women would just have taken the dead child as hers because all babies look alike, but this woman had the diligence and observation to know they were different. Diligently she was living; diligently she examined. You may not approve of her profession but you can certainly applaud her sense of diligence. She was a very careful and caring woman.

The third thing about her is that she acted in the morning while the other one acted at night. **She acted in the light.** She was sincere, not secretive. She was not scheming; she was sincere. Her actions were in the light, and if you look at it there are two kinds of light associated with her: the dawn light and the early morning light. She woke up at dawn to feed her child. She saw the child was dead, but she didn't make a decision. She said 'let me wait for a greater light because I need to properly examine this in order to make a decision.' And when she examined in the morning she realized that it was not her child lying dead next to her.

There are people who make decisions with the dawn light; with just a little light and they don't wait for a greater light to have a clearer picture to make a decision. Wisdom does not make a decision at dawn; wisdom makes a decision in the full light of the morning. Wisdom waits until they have a broader picture, more light, a greater understanding to be able to tell whether what they have is theirs or not.

This was a wise woman. So of these two, which one is you? The question is not only for the women, but for the men also. Which one are you? Are you the reckless one who is destroying yours and stealing what someone else has? Are you the wise one who is preserving and diligently protecting what you have?

**The Mothers' Test**

When these two women brought their case to Solomon, Solomon put them to a test by giving them two options.

*The first test was to kill the living.* Solomon suggested they should divide the living child and give half to each woman. Since they were both fighting over the living child Solomon wanted each one to have a fair and equal piece of what they were fighting for. The only thing was that if they had a piece of what they were fighting for they would kill the child that they both wanted.

*The second test was to share the dead.* Solomon's second option was to give each mother a piece of a dead child. He offered to provide them a half of something they couldn't use. Whenever we are fighting over something we have to think about Solomon's test. Are we going to fail this test or pass it? Will we kill the living and share the dead? Many times, indeed we do kill the living and share the dead. It happens in marriages; we kill a living marriage just enjoy a dead one. We kill a living business and share the dead. In our effort to fight for something we have to be careful we are not killing the living just to enjoy the booty of what is dead. Some victories are not worth the fight, because, yes, you may win, but you must think ahead of time whether what you have won is not just a half dead child. You may have won the debate but what did you really gain? You fought and fought and won, but what did you get?

Solomon says, "I'm going to kill this child and both of you will have nothing; you are going to just share the dead." There were two responses to Solomon's test.

## The Destroyer's Logic

The first woman had what I call the destroyer's logic. The destroyer's logic says *if I can't have it, then nobody else will have it either. I would rather destroy it.* You often hear this; it is the language and attitude in power struggles. You hear it in relationships, for example between a boyfriend and a girlfriend. The boyfriend says, *if you don't marry me, then nobody else will marry you, so I'm going to destroy your reputation so nobody else can marry you.* The girl says, *if you won't marry me then I'm going to destroy you and make sure nobody marries you.*

You also hear such power struggles in the workplace, for example, with industrial actions and strikes. People go on strike and destroy the property that feeds them. I heard about some students who went on strike and burnt their school down. I wondered to myself, where do they plan to go for classes after the strike is over? Workers have destroyed factories they work for, but did they think about where they would work after the strike was over?

People destroy their potential spouses and say the most horrible things about them. But what happens when the problem is resolved? Who do you marry? Will you marry the woman that you told everybody bad things about, or the man that you insulted to everyone? The destroyer's logic says, if I cannot have it, I'm going to destroy it for everybody else.

I truly hope you never have that logic. I hope that is not your language. The destroyer's logic also says, *I want it even if it will not benefit me*. That is what this woman said. She was okay with going ahead, dividing the baby, and taking a dead half of the child. Wisdom would ask, what do you want a half dead child for? A dead body divided in two; what would you do with it? You cannot play with it; you cannot raise it, so what would you do with it? Would you eat it, would you burry it, would you cuddle it? There is no useful purpose for half of a dead child but she chose that option. It is amazing the kinds of things people want!

Those who want what other people have at all cost speak the language of envy and selfishness. They do not care about the damage they cause to others, and they aren't concerned with whether what they are fighting for will benefit them. All they want is what the other person has, and even if it will in no way benefit them, they still want it. That's not the voice of wisdom.

Many of people among us are fighting for things that are useless; fighting for property that won't truly benefit us. They may have everything, but still want the little that somebody else has, just in order to take it from them. Even if it will destroy them, they do not care. Even if it will not benefit them; it doesn't matter; they just want it to make sure the other person doesn't get it.

## The Preserver's Logic

The wise woman on the other hand, had what I call the preserver's logic. Remember, wisdom is a builder; foolishness is the one that destroys. The builder's logic says *though I can't have it, I still want it to live*. It is a language of compassion, and unfortunately not many people speak this language. You can only speak this language when you are mature, and in my adult life, only a small percent of the people I've come across speak this language. It is rare to find someone who would say, *yes, I want it, and although I can't have it, let it live*. I cannot have it, but it deserves another opportunity. I cannot marry her, but I still want her to have peace and joy with somebody else. I cannot marry him, but he still deserves to enjoy a full life with somebody else. The relationship didn't go on well, and he proposed to me and changed his mind, but it's okay, may he find the woman that is right for him. Only a few people can talk this way; probably five to ten percent. The majority will say, divide the baby! The voice of the preserver says, even though I have a right to it, I sacrifice my right so I can preserve what I love. This is the language of one who nurtures, one who has a sense of ownership, compassion and responsibility.

The wise mother saw the life of her child as more important than her right to claim motherhood. Yes, she was the mother; yes, she gave birth to the child; yes, she had dreams for her child; yes, she was right. But what is a dead child to my dreams? It is like the mother of Moses who couldn't give him up to be destroyed and said, *rather than destroy my child, I'd rather let somebody else mother him.* Then she put this child Moses, on the Nile River, for him to be discovered by somebody else. I can imagine the years of agony knowing he was her child, while somebody else claimed him, nurtured him and enjoyed him calling her 'mother.' For forty years, she must have been screaming inside, saying, *that's my child!* but one day that child came back to her as a redeemer, all because she gave up her right for what she loved.

Let me just say this: if you are going to be wise, it is not about going to school; it is about whether you preserve or you destroy. If that relationship has gone bad, the decisive question is, are you going to destroy that man, are you going to destroy that woman? If your marriage is not going well, the decisive question to reveal your wisdom is, are you going to destroy your husband before his children, are you going destroy your wife before her children just so you can win the argument or cover up your own wrongdoings? Wisdom doesn't think that way. Wisdom says, *I know I may be right and my spouse did bad things, but rather than destroying my children's relationship with their father or with their mother, I will do whatever it takes for that relationship to live.* Are you ready to let it live?

There are people who leave places and in leaving, he wants to destroy what he is leaving. Sometimes it happens in the church. A pastor feels he must move on because he is not happy where he is. But as he is going he attempts to destroy the congregation so that everybody can say that when he left nothing worked. Such a person does not apply wisdom to recognize that when you destroy the congregation, you are not just winning a case; you are destroying peoples' faith and commitment to God, because people believe pastors are honest and sincere, and here you are, behaving like a crude unbeliever. You may harm somebody eternally.

There comes a time when you must rise above winning the argument; you have to choose instead to let the baby live. Move on, but let the baby live. That's the voice of wisdom. Wisdom builds, foolishness tears down.

So consider all the things you are fighting for: in your office; at home; in your family relationships; you and your brother; you and your sister; you and your cousins; consider what you are fighting for; is it worth it? Are you going to have a half baby left? Are you splitting the family in two? Think about what you will truly walk away with. What will you really get? Yes, you may win, but what exactly will you achieve? A split family; a split relationship; a destroyed business; a destroyed church; a destroyed nation; a destroyed community after you won your case. The one who says, *I'm right, but I want the baby to live,* that's a wise person because wisdom builds her house and she preserves it. Wisdom does not orchestrate the demolition of what she has painfully built.

Allow me to counsel you; if you are in the process of destroying something that has been built, think again. You are probably hurt, you are probably disappointed, you've been mistreated, you've been wrongly accused, and you've been given a dead baby. Just pause and ask yourself, is that hurt big enough for you to destroy everything?

Are you one of those people who will say, *when I leave from here, fire will burn everything to the ground?* I have felt that way before. I think all of us have. When my father died, it was just about a year after my mum had died. I was a teenager and I remember it so well. His relatives came to our home and they took everything away. Everything. They came while there was nobody in the house, and they took everything of the little we had, and left me. I was alone in the house because all my siblings had been distributed to relatives and I was the only one in the house. They took everything.

Not long ago, the chief of my father's village along with the elders of the village came to my office here in Accra with a goat to thank me because I had sunk a borehole for them that supplied them with water for the first time in that village. Yes, I know what they did was wrong, but that's why we serve an awesome God. He's able to give you far more than what you have lost. If you do not let bitterness lead you to destroying people, God will give you far more than what you gave up because wisdom will always prevail and win.

## Something Greater

By the three biblical figures we have examined, we can say Solomon was indeed a wise man, but how does Jesus Himself describe the wisdom we have in Him? In Luke 11:31 Jesus is rebuking the people of His time and listen to how He puts it:

> *The queen of the South will rise up in the judgement with the men of this generation and condemn them, for she came from the ends of the earth to hear the wisdom of Solomon; and indeed a greater than Solomon is here.*

In the New King James Version it says 'a greater' but in the original Greek it says, 'something greater'.

The NIV renders it clearer. It says,

> *The queen of the South will rise at the judgement with the people of this generation and condemn them, for she came from the ends of the earth to listen to Solomon's wisdom, and now, something greater than Solomon is here.*

What or who is that 'something greater than Solomon' the Scripture speaks of? It is Jesus! It is not just Jesus as a person alone, like Solomon, because the wisdom of Christ is higher than Solomon's wisdom. Solomon's wisdom was great, but it did not stop him from acting foolishly. He was a man of wisdom and wrote about wisdom, but he ended up marrying seven hundred wives and having three hundred concubines. If that is not the height of foolishness, I don't know what that is!

Solomon was the one who warned people about the adulterous woman, and then married her himself. Solomon told people if you pick an adulterous woman in your bosom it is like fire; it is going to burn you, but he married seven hundred of them. Solomon's wisdom was not pure. It was good wisdom, and we can learn from it, but there is wisdom greater than Solomon and His name is Jesus.

When Solomon prayed for wisdom, he did not pray for wisdom for his personal life. When God asked him what he wanted, he said, *I want wisdom*; but what he wanted to use the wisdom for was to rule the people. He didn't say *I want wisdom to guide my life*. Solomon's wisdom was professional but it was not personal.

There are people with great professional wisdom. People who run great companies often have great professional wisdom, but their lives are a mess. How can a man who makes brilliant decisions in the boardroom make such silly decisions in his private life? They have Solomon's wisdom. Solomon didn't apply his wisdom internally; he used it only for his public-facing life.

The wisdom of Christ is higher than Solomon's wisdom.

Contrary to Solomon's wisdom, the wisdom of Christ works from your inside and makes its presence visible to the outside. It changes you from within before you see it externally. A greater than Solomon is here.

***The kingdom of God is greater than Solomon's kingdom.*** The kingdom of God that Christ came to establish is greater than Solomon's kingdom. Solomon's kingdom was built on compromise. He did not fight battles; he did not grow his kingdom by conquests, he grew his kingdom by compromise. One of the reasons Solomon married seven hundred wives was to enter into political alliance with other nations. Whereas David grew his kingdom by fighting, Solomon grew his kingdom by compromising. In order to make other people nice to him, Solomon married everybody that God said he should not marry. However, in the kingdom of God we do not compromise for greatness. We stand on the truth and God promotes us because we honour Him. The kingdom of God is greater than Solomon's kingdom.

***The glory of Christ is superior to Solomon's glory.*** Solomon's glory was in riches and material possessions. Christ's glory is spiritual. The kingdom of God is not meat and drink, but righteousness, peace and joy in the Holy Spirit. Something greater than Solomon is here for us now.

That is why as Christians when we are praying for wisdom we do not say, *God, give me the wisdom of Solomon*. No, we have something far better; we have the wisdom of Christ.

For of Him are you in Christ who has been made to us wisdom5. If you want to be wise there are many people who can inspire you and challenge you, but the greatest role model you can have is the source of wisdom – Jesus Christ – the One whose wisdom is greater than Solomon's.

If you ask Him to come into your heart, then wisdom will come to live inside you, and guide you. If you listen to Him, you may be foolish now, but you will grow in wisdom. You may be base now, but you will be strong; you may be weak but you will be mighty if you accept the wisdom of Christ. You may be despised, but He'll lift you up because His wisdom will transport you from the lowest level of life and lift you to a place of glory and honour.

That is what the wisdom of God does. As we remember the birth of Jesus, His incarnation, when He took on flesh, it gives us a great opportunity to receive the wisdom of God in our lives. Jesus came and paid the price. You do not need to go to hell. You do not need to be punished or to die for your sins because He paid it all. All you need to do is to say, *Lord Jesus, I thank You for what You did for me and I ask You to come into my life.*

As simple as that is, God has chosen such a simple step to bring salvation to mankind. There are people paying money for salvation and travelling on long pilgrimages. There are people chasing all kinds of things for salvation; people drink anointing oil and holy oil and get sprinkled in it for salvation. There are people praying on little hills and mountains for salvation. People do all kinds of things and travel all over the world, but the way is very simple. God has chosen the foolish things of this world to put to shame the wisdom of men.

The way of the cross is the wisdom of God and when you accept Jesus into your life, He changes your life because the Bible says, *old things will pass away and all thing will become new.*[6]

Today is a good day to be saved. Today is a good day to be born again. Today is a good day for Jesus to come into your heart. Today is a good day for salvation to enter you. Today is a good day to say, *today, I receive Jesus into my heart and I ask him to be my wisdom.*

There are people who go to church and think, *since I go to church, I have salvation. And since I go to Otabil's church, then I know I'm really a Christian.* I wish that was so, but coming to my church does not make you a Christian. My own faith is not in myself, it is in Jesus. So if my faith is in Jesus, then your faith should not be in me because I cannot save you. My faith is in Jesus, and your faith should be in Jesus Christ also. He is the one who saved me by His shed blood, died for me on the cross, rose again. The One I put my faith in is the one who saved me from my sins, and he is the only One who can save you

If you want to have what I have, then you should get the wisdom that I have – Jesus. It is not about attending church. It is not about having a wristband or a church cloth; it is not even about reading your Bible. It is nice to have a church cloth that we can all wear to church but that does not give you salvation. Salvation is not in a church cloth; it is not in a devotional guide; salvation is a Man and His name is Jesus and you must receive Him into your heart. It is the only way to receive the wisdom of God.

CHAPTER

*07*

# WISDOM IN OUR LIVES

Proverbs 24:30-34 is an interesting passage of Scripture, one that I want to focus on in this chapter, starting by highlight how it says wisdom develops.

It reads:

> *I went by the field of the lazy man, and by the vineyard of the man devoid of understanding; and there it was, all overgrown with thorns; its surface was covered with nettles; its stone wall was broken down. When I saw it, I considered it well; I looked on it and received instruction: a little sleep, a little slumber, a little folding of the hands to rest; so shall your poverty come like a prowler, and your need like an armed man.*

## How Wisdom Develops

First, let's look at how the scripture says wisdom develops. As I studied this passage, I gleaned four ways in which it tells us that wisdom develops.

- **By casual introduction.** In verse one it says, *I went by the field of the lazy man.* Although the fact that it is the field of the lazy man and the vineyard of the man devoid of understanding seems to be the key point there, I want us to look closer at the phrase *I went by.* "I went by" gives the impression of a casual passing. Many times wisdom does not rush in to reveal itself to us. Sometimes it comes to us like a casual stroll. Sometimes as we are just passing through life, just looking at things without any serious intention, and that is when a great revelation or understanding comes to us. Often times, our introduction to wisdom is casual. That is when something is brought to our attention, even though we are not looking for it or focused on finding answers to any particular question in life.

- **Through keen observation.** The casual introduction is important to note, but let us back up to where the passage starts. It says, "I went by the field of the lazy man, *and I saw it.*" The verse tells us that the field was run down, overgrown and its walls were broken down. This is the image of decay. We've all seen places like that, and it is easy to just pass by without learning anything from it. You would assume there is nothing to learn, or at least, nothing useful to learn from it. The passage adds, *and I saw it.* That phrase indicates keen observation, which is another way wisdom can develop. When you pay attention to what you are looking at it opens the door for wisdom to come in. When you pass by something that has the potential to give you wisdom, unless you home in on it, you might overlook it.

- **By deep examination**. Then, the passage says, *I considered it well.* This means he took time to gain a deeper understanding through further examination. In life, something may grab your attention and cause you to notice something you had not considered before. As you continue to think about it, question it, and look at it from different angles, your understanding of the deeper principles it reveals can give you greater wisdom.

- **Through personal application.** The fourth thing he says in the passage is, *I received instruction.* When you observe and examine something, wisdom will tell you to act on it. That is what you must do after you have casually come upon something, taken time to look at it closely and examined it. From all the information you have gathered, wisdom will speak to you about what to do with that new knowledge. It will tell you to apply it.

What then was the conclusion the writer drew from what he had observed? He concluded that laziness will invite poverty into your life, and it will not be subtle. He said it will come like a prowler and the lack of what you need will attack you like an armed man. Have you ever felt that poverty is chasing you like an armed robber? If so, then this passage is talking to you. It is advising you that if you sleep and slumber, if you do not get to work, your field will overgrow with weeds and thorns, and poverty will pounce on your life.

This passage is a reminder that we do not gain wisdom by pressuring ourselves to be wise. Gaining wisdom is not like cramming for an exam. You cannot just squeeze your face, and channel wisdom into yourself. Wisdom comes to us more delicately. First it starts by just walking by and speaking to our observation. What the writer of this passage is saying is that wisdom is all around us. Just as you walk around, take time to pay attention. Deeply examine what you see and you will find instruction; you will learn wisdom.

God gives us frequent opportunity to gain wisdom. Somebody's experience can make you wise. Somebody's calamity can make you wise. When you hear somebody's marriage is having problems, do not gossip about it; examine it and take counsel. Learn from it so that your marriage will be better. When you hear something bad has happened to somebody, you should remember this passage. Walk by it, really see what it reveals, pay attention, examine it and learn.

Many times people say that experience is the best teacher, but sometimes experience is not a teacher. Some experiences are killers. You cannot learn from what destroys you. Someone else can learn from it, but if it is your experience, what it teaches, you cannot learn. Experience is not necessarily the best teacher. However, other people's experience can teach you a great deal. That is how wisdom develops. It comes when we look at what is happening in other people's lives, when we examine it deeply and we advise ourselves.

When you see things happening to people, learn from it so you can avoid it happening to you first hand. Don't push yourself to go through what everybody else is going through. Learn from the difficulty they go through, you do not need to go through it. You can learn, you can observe and you can take counsel.

Wisdom is very important. I like what Job 11:12 says:

> *For an empty-headed man will be wise, when a wild donkey's colt is born a man.*

Of course, we all know that a wild donkey does not give birth to a human being. It just cannot happen. Job tells us that the likelihood of a donkey giving birth to a human is the same likelihood of an empty-headed man having wisdom. It is not going to happen. In other words, it is impossible.

What Job is telling us is that if you do not apply your mind to observe, think consider, question and examine, you will never be wise. Wisdom doesn't just drop on your head. Vow to yourself that you will not be empty-headed. Use your mind; use your brain; encounter knowledge and information, then wisdom will be born in your heart.

## The Anatomy of Wisdom

As I stated previously, wisdom is not an easy concept to define. Thus far, we have used different analogies and frameworks to develop our understanding of wisdom. One analogy that I think is very insightful is to look at wisdom through the prism of different body parts, and how they function. In this manner, let us walk through the anatomy of wisdom, looking at the heart, the ears, the lips, the eyes and the face of wisdom. We will start with the wise heart.

### The Wise Heart

*The wise heart is upright and virtuous.*

Where is the heart of wisdom? The heart of wisdom is set in uprightness and virtue. Ecclesiastes 10:2 tells us that a wise person's heart is upright and virtuous, as it says:

> *A wise man's heart is at his right hand, but a fool's heart at his left.*

We all know biologically that every human being's heart is on the left side of the body, but this passage is not speaking from a biological perspective. It is a metaphor. In the Hebrew culture the right hand always stands for uprightness. It represents being virtuous and having favour. The left hand represents crookedness and dishonour.

Remember Jesus said that in the kingdom of heaven the sheep will go to the right hand and the goats will go to the left hand? He said this because in the culture of the Hebrews, and still in many cultures today, the left hand is seen as being crooked or not upright and the right hand is seen as virtuous and upright.

The verse says the heart of the wise man is on the right side. It means the heart of the wise man is upright and virtuous. It is not talking about the biological heart; it is talking about the values deep in your heart; the things that are very important to you, and are at the core of the wise man's heart – the right hand.

In order to be wise, you will need to have deep values, to be virtuous, and to be upright. It is not possible to be crooked and be wise. That is the wisdom of the world, but the wisdom of God is upright; it is pure, it is holy, it is righteous; it is on the right side.

### *The wise heart has depth.*

The second thing about the heart of the wise man, is that not only is his heart upright, but the heart of the wise man is deep. Wise people are not shallow. They have depth and they operate in deep things. Proverbs 20:5 says,

> *Counsel in the heart of man is like deep water, But a man of understanding will draw it out.*

Wise people see beyond what lies on the surface and they offer fresh insights; they are never dry. A wise person will always bring something interesting to the discussion. They will always bring new ideas, new revelation, new thoughts, and new perspectives. The wise man's heart is deep. The question everyone must ask himself or herself is, is my heart deep? Are you a shallow person? What are the things that you talk about? What are the things that interest you? What are the things that you really want to spend time to know about? Do you want to know about people's outfits? It's good to know about popular fashion, if you are a clothing designer. If you are a clothing designer, then it is good to study your industry and what other designers are doing and what people are wearing. But if you are not a clothing designer or professional fashion editor and you spend hours just talking about what someone was wearing, your heart has a problem. There's no depth.

For many of us, all that we look for are surface things that have no depth that have no depth of meaning in life. A wise man's heart is deep; has depth and is not shallow.

### *The wise heart is humble.*

Third thing about a wise person's heart is that it is not over confident. Proverbs 28:26 says:

> *He who trusts in his own heart is a fool, But whoever walks wisely will be delivered.*

The fool is a person whom the Bible describes as full of himself, and the Book of Proverbs has a lot of advice for people who are overconfident and who are wise in their own eyes. A wise person's heart is not overconfident. A wise person does not think themselves better than other people. A wise person, even if they are very good at something, even if they are the best in their field, they still think that other people have value and something to contribute, and they never lift themselves up above everybody else.

If you think you are the best in the whole world, then you are not wise. If you think there is nobody like you, you are not wise. If you think you are the wisest person in the world, guess what, you just became the most unwise person in the world because the wise person's heart is not lifted up in pride and arrogance. The wise person's heart is humble.

Do you have a humble heart? Do you respect other people's opinion? Do you listen to other people? Do you think others have something to contribute? If that is your attitude in life, and that is your heart and that is how you see life then you have the beginnings of wisdom. But if you think you are smarter than everyone else, your heart is on the path to foolishness.

The person who always thinks elevated and haughty will be brought down, according to scripture. A wise person's heart is humble; it is deep and is in the right place, it is upright.

**Wise Ears**

The second thing we want to look at, apart from the heart of the wise is the ear of the wise person. There are a few characteristics of a wise person's ear that we should note.

*Wise ears seek knowledge and understanding.*

The first thing about a wise person's ear is that it seeks knowledge and understanding. The wise person's ear is listening for knowledge. The wise person's ear is always open to knowledge and understanding. They want to learn new things and become better.

Proverbs 1:5 says:

> *A wise man will hear and increase learning, and a man of understanding will attain wise counsel.*

A wise man will hear and increase learning. Do you hear to increase learning? Can you say that the knowledge stock you have gained this year is higher than the knowledge stock you had last year? Has your knowledge increased from last year to this year? Did you learn new things? This month have you learnt something better than what you knew last month? If you haven't, then you do not have the ear of the wise, because the ear of the wise is open to knowledge. It means the wise person is going to listen to things that bring knowledge.

If they turn on the television, they are going to turn on to a channel that gives them knowledge; not a channel that just makes them dance, because there's no knowledge in it. It's pretty safe to say that most Africans like dancing, and don't get me wrong, when I say that because it is good to dance; but we dance for everything. If we are playing football, we dance; if the President is returning home from diplomatic travels, we are dancing; when the government is going to present the budget, we are dancing; when the budget is closed, we are dancing. A child is born, we are dancing; he dies, we are dancing. We are always dancing. Can we not stop dancing and start listening? We don't have time to ponder life, to think, to analyze and to be serious. Sometimes we want life to be too much fun.

A wise person's ear is open to knowledge. What television stations do you listen to? Which is your favourite television programme? What is your favourite radio programme? What is your favourite section in the newspapers? What do you read frequently? Does it increase your knowledge? If it doesn't, then I have to tell you something; the Bible describes you many times. It says you are not wise. If you were wise you would open your ear to knowledge. You would attend seminars, workshops and retreats. When you hear there is a lecture going on somewhere you are going to listen because the ear of the wise man increases knowledge.

**Wise ears receive correction.**

The second thing about the ear of the wise person is that their ear is able to handle correction. Not only is his ear open to knowledge, but also the wise person's ear can handle correction. They can handle rebuke. They aren't fragile when they receive critique. They don't want to only hear sweet things; they want to hear things that will help them grow. When you tell them about their mistakes, their ears are open. Proverbs 15:31-32 says:

> *The ear that hears the rebukes of life will abide among the wise. He who disdains instruction despises his own soul, but he who heeds rebuke gets understanding.*

The wise person doesn't get offended when they are rebuked. There are people who cannot handle correction. They get offended; they get hurt and there may be many reasons, but sometimes the reason is that they were never corrected when they were young. There are people who were never corrected; nobody told them they were wrong. Nobody told them "No;" nobody told them "don't do that;" nobody told them "that's a mistake." Because sometimes, depending on which family you came from, you can grow up in a family where children are never rebuked. The toffee table is there, they say, "take one," but the child takes two and nobody rebukes them. They throw tantrums, nobody rebukes them; they push their food away, nobody rebukes them; they insult a neighbor, nobody rebukes them; they insult their brother or sister, nobody rebukes them; they use bad words, nobody rebukes them, so they grow up thinking that they are perfect and right and nobody has a right to rebuke them. Some people when you rebuke them later in life, they tell you that even their mother and father didn't rebuke them. That's why they are rotten, by the way.

There are people who cannot handle rebuke, but the wise man's ear is not just waiting for endorsement and praise. The wise man's ear says, *thank you for correcting me when you saw my mistake. I appreciate that you told me the mistake because I'm not interested in thinking that I am always right, I am focused on growing and always getting better.* Because the Bible says when you do that you dwell amongst the wise.

There are also some people who have been rebuked all their life; they've been over-rebuked. They've had more than their full share of rebuke so when those type of people grow up, they don't want anybody to rebuke them again because they've had a lifetime of correction. Anytime you correct them, they get angry, because it reminds them of a father or mother, or somebody who was always shutting them up, so they rebel against rebuke. These are two extremes: those who were never rebuked and those who were over-rebuked. Both of them need help and may struggle to get wisdom, but the wise man's ear is open to correction. Don't quit your job because somebody rebuked you; don't be angry because your friend rebuked you, or your husband said something about your cooking, so you won't cook again. Go back to work and learn from the correction. Hear your friend out and continue your friendship. Cook, but do it better. The same goes for husbands too. When you buy her a new shoe and it is the wrong size, don't get angry because she never wears a shoe that doesn't fit her. Take note of her shoe size and try again with better wisdom.

### Wise ears are discerning.

Thirdly, the wise man's ear diligently weighs what is heard. Wise people don't jump to conclusions. They don't act on hearsay. Proverbs 18:13:

> *He who answers a matter before he hears it, it is folly and shame to him.*

It is foolishness not to have a better view of an issue before you decide. You cannot just hear one part, or assumed something, or you hear an insinuation, or you thought it, and based on that you take a position. It is not wise. The Bible says it is folly, because if you are wise, your ears are going to open. You will say, *well, I thought it was like this, but what is it really about?* Or *I heard this side, but what is the other side?* A wise person's ears are open to other facts, perspectives and opinions. They weigh what they hear. They don't answer; they don't draw conclusions based on undeveloped views because in this world if you don't diligently weigh what you hear, you are going to hear things that can steer you wayward and bruise your soul. Sometimes, it is not the full truth.

Have you heard people when they are recounting what somebody said and they add elements that you know people don't typically use when they speak? The person tells you, he said, *ehhhh, you're like this and like that*. I wonder, who really says *ehhhhh* when he is speaking? It's usually only in reporting that we add *ehhhhhhs* and other decorations to it, which gives it a certain colouration as if the person was disrespecting you when they made the statement. So find out yourself what was said. The wise man's ear weighs diligently what it hears. It is unwise for you to draw conclusions simply because somebody gave you a little view without getting the whole picture. The ear of the wise diligently weighs what is heard.

**Wise lips**

What do the lips of the wise look like? When we talk about the lips here, we are using it in the sense of speaking. The lips of the wise deals with what wise people say; their words; what is expressed verbally.

*Wise lips make intelligent contributions.*

The first thing about the lips of the wise is that they make intelligent contributions. Proverbs 16:21 says:

*The wise in heart will be called prudent, and sweetness of the lips increases learning.*

When a wise person speaks it is measured; it is wise; it is well managed; it is prudent and it adds more learning. It helps people to be more knowledgeable, it gives further information, and it brings enlightenment. When a wise person is in a meeting they seek to add to the discussion. They seek to increase the group's understanding of the problems they are discussing. Proverbs 15:7 says:

*The lips of the wise disperse knowledge, but the heart of the fool does not do so.*

*Wise lips disperse knowledge.*

When a wise person is in a meeting and it is their turn to make a contribution, they talk with sense. Wise people don't sit in a meeting and when their opinion is asked, they just go off on a tangent. Only a non-wise person will do that, and everybody will be wondering, *what was he thinking?* Sometimes people sit in meetings and their mind is somewhere else; it has travelled, and so a point is being discussed and they are not mentally present so when someone asks them, *so what do you think?* they answer anyhow and those at the meeting are trying to help make sense of the comment because you were lost. The lips of the wise man at a meeting, helps the meeting. It increases knowledge. If you are going to speak, speak wisdom. If you have nothing to say, it is wise to keep quiet.

Have you ever been at a meeting where you made a contribution, stated your mind about something and you just knew that what you said was not sensible? Has it happened to you before? You stated your point and your point was confusing even to yourself as you stated the point, and you finish the point and you just wish you hadn't said anything. At that time, foolishness became your neighbor but the lips of the wise man increases learning. So next time you are at a meeting and your opinion is called, think about this book and choose wisdom. One of the best ways to be wise is to let your words be few. Because when your words are few, even when it is not sensible, it is short and people don't remember it much. But when it is long and not sensible, you prolong the pain. The lips of the wise make intelligent contributions.

### Wise lips carefully manage information.

When you are a wise person you just don't talk, as we say in Ghana, by heart. You don't just speak without thinking. You carefully manage knowledge. Proverbs 15:2 says:

> *The tongue of the wise uses knowledge rightly, but the mouth of fools pours forth foolishness.*

### Wise lips use knowledge rightly.

This means there is a way in which you can use knowledge wrongly. The wise person's words use knowledge rightly. They use information rightly. They do not use information just because they have it. There are some people who just say everything; anything that comes to mind, they say it. A wise person must know how to use privileged information. Privileged information is any information that comes to your attention because of privileged access, especially when you are in a position of confidence.

I am a pastor; I'm in a position of confidence and because I'm a pastor people trust me, and they tell me things. You will be amazed sometimes what people tell pastors. They just talk about their lives, talk about their secrets and sometimes talk about things that are very weighty. Now, that's knowledge given to me. The Bible says my lips must use that knowledge rightly because if I don't use that knowledge rightly, I can damage the person who gave me that knowledge. If I'm doing marriage counselling, I get information. Sometimes husbands tell me things about their wives and wives tell me things about their husbands. That's knowledge. I have to use it wisely.

If a man is frustrated with his wife, and he's talking to me and he says, *pastor, my wife is not beautiful; look at the way she's grown so fat and even when I see her, it makes me angry.* That's knowledge. Now, when I'm talking to the wife, I cannot say, *yesterday, you should have been here! Your husband eiiiiiiiiiiii, he says you are fat like a caterpillar!* I have knowledge, but what am I doing? I'm not using my lips rightly. I'm not managing that information. Instead, I should say, *I spoke to your husband, he has some concerns about you and I think the two of you should sit together and I really want to help you to manage this.* That is using that information rightly. I don't go repeating things raw.

The wise man's lips use information rightly. If you are a friend you have to manage information rightly between two friends, because friends get upset and they can say nasty things about the other person, to your hearing. Don't go to the other person and say, as for me I tell the truth; I can't lie; whatever he says, I'm telling you the truth; this is the way he said it. Yes, you may have said it, you've repeated the information, but you are not wise, because a wise person's lips rightly manages knowledge. Even though it has come to your attention, your lips must manage it well.

Sometimes, because of our positions, if you are a doctor or nurse, a lot of information will come to you about peoples' health. You don't leave the hospital and say, *eiiii, this man, the disease he has will kill him very soon*. It's not wise. Wisdom rightly manages knowledge.

**Wise lips don't speak rashly.**

The third thing about the lips of a wise man is that they don't speak rashly. Proverbs 10:19 says,

> *In the multitude of words sin is not lacking, but he who restrains his lips is wise.*

Here, the Bible is simply saying that if you talk and talk and talk, you will inevitably say the wrong thing. A wise person measures what he or she says. They practice the art of using a few words to say a lot. They avoid the temptation to respond to everything that they hear.

Proverbs 17:28 goes on to say,

> *Even a fool is counted wise when he holds his peace; when he shuts his lips, he is considered perceptive.*

Many times people feel they must have an answer for everything, even if they don't know the answer. However, keeping quiet will make you look wise; it will help your image.

Now, I understand that there are people who are outgoing and who have sunny personalities and they are the life of a party; wherever they are, they make everybody happy, they crack jokes and therefore they talk a lot. That's their personality and I'm not saying that it is wrong. It doesn't mean that now you should go and keep quiet all the time. People will think you are sick if you all of a sudden become quiet and subdued because they know you to be a happy and outgoing person. Instead, the question is, how can somebody be a happy person, who talks a lot, is outgoing and still be wise? Wisdom is not only found in introverted people; it doesn't mean extroverted people are not wise, you can be extroverted and wise and you can be introverted and not wise. It's all about how you manage information. The Bible says you don't speak rashly. Talkative people can continue to be themselves, but they should just be careful not to speak rashly.

Let me give you a few ideas that will help you if you are an outgoing person and you don't want your words to sin:

- **Learn to pause when you speak.** When you are talking, pause somewhere. Give yourself time and think. God gave us two ears, yet only one mouth. The wisdom I see in that is that we should listen twice as much as we speak. You don't talk more than what you hear. So when you are talking give opportunity for hearing. If you are a person who is outgoing, you talk a lot, you are always expressing yourself, learn to put pauses in your speeches, in what you are saying.

- **Learn to allow other people the opportunity to also speak.** Give people space and one of the best ways to do that, if you are a person who speaks a lot, who is outgoing, is that instead of always expressing an opinion,

- **Learn to ask questions.** When you ask a question you are inviting other people to speak, but when you are always offering an opinion, you are shutting everybody up. So those of you who are outgoing, who speak a lot, add questions to your conversations and invite others to speak. If you don't ask questions and you are always the one talking, it will increase the chance of sinning with your lips. Pretty soon you will say something wrong and end up offending people.

Take care with your lips; measure what you say, put pauses, allow other people space and ask questions as a way of managing your personality not to hinder you. By all means, remain your happy self. The whole world cannot be full of quiet people, like me. I can go to a party or meeting and sit down and watch because I'm studying everybody and I'm taking counsel, watching everybody and learning. That's my personality. I only talk a lot when I'm preaching because I've listened for the week and now I can preach. But there are people who talk all the time. I like people who talk because I don't talk, but if you talk and you are expressive, you have to learn to manage it well otherwise you will create offenses and it is not good for you because it will lower your own self confidence. Don't speak rashly.

### Wise lips do not speak deceitfully.

The lips of the wise man do not speak deceitfully. Proverbs 4:24 says,

> *Put away from you a deceitful mouth, and put perverse lips far from you.*

Simply put, the Bible is saying, tell the truth; don't twist facts; don't over-embellish or exaggerate things. There is a certain measure of exaggeration that is normal to every reported speech, but then there is an over-exaggeration that gives a totally distorted meaning and sometimes it becomes a truthful lie so if you have the lips of a wise person, you don't speak deceitfully, you don't deceive people, you don't tell them the wrong thing, you don't speak with the intention of entrapping people.

I like what Proverbs 18:6 says:

> *A fool's lips enter into contention, and his mouth calls for blows.*

Sometimes when I read this I wonder how it got into the Bible. The Bible is supposed to be a very holy book, but it tells us that a fool's lips enter into contention, and his mouth calls for blows. Some peoples' mouths are inviting blows, calling out, "Beat me." You know, there are people who leave home very well dressed and often return with a swollen mouth. Because somehow, in the midst of the day, they pick a fight, and how did they pick a fight? With their mouth's invitation, 'hit me; beat me.' They come home having been slapped around, not because they stole, but because they spoke wrongly.

Some people can be crossed by another car in the traffic; their car wasn't hit and there was no damage, but they simply cannot move on. Instead, they feel they must park by the roadside, get out of the car, and release their mouth to invite blows. I see it in our city sometimes and I marvel.

The person gets beaten and people come and separate the two fighting, yet the mouthy one continues threatening the other. His shirt is torn, there's blood on his lips, and he's angry. What fascinates me is what he does next. He just gets back into his car and continues the journey. I just wonder about such a person, because if after the fight he was able to just drive off to his original destination, then why this interlude? People with this character, should always read Proverbs 18:6.

### The Eyes of the Wise

There are several things the Scripture points out about how the eyes of the wise function.

*The eyes of the wise are not greedy for wealth.*

First, the eye of the wise is not greedy for wealth. Proverbs 28:22 says:

> *A man with an evil eye hastens after riches, and does not consider that poverty will come upon him.*

An evil eye in this context is a greedy eye. The Bible says it hastens after riches and it always ends up in poverty. A wise person does not allow their eye to roam with greed, always looking for what they can gain. That kind of eye can cause you to make bad decisions that can cost you.

*The eyes of the wise are not focused on what others have.*

Secondly the eye of the wise person is not focused on what other people have. It is not always seeking to possess what it sees. The wise person does not have the attitude that if somebody has it, I must have it also. This verse tells us that if you do that you will impoverish your own soul.

Many of the problems people have in life is not really because of necessity; it has to do with greed; greed for money; greed for what someone else has, and we have to deal with that; whether it is greed for other peoples' wives, greed for other peoples' husbands, greed for other women apart from your wife, greed for other men apart from your husband. It's greed, and the wise person must have a covenant with his eye, like Job said. Job said I've signed a covenant with my eyes; I will not look at a woman twice.

Before I married, I signed that covenant that I will not look at a woman twice. In those days I was a very young man and when I'm going out and I see a woman, and my mind says 'look at her again', I say no, no, no, and I look straight. There's only one woman I looked at twice, and then I had to marry her and now I look at her all the time. You have to discipline your eyes; discipline yourself.

Our walk with God is about discipline. Discipline is bringing your body into order and making your body do what it must do and not what it wants to do. You have to discipline your eyes. Part of that is disciplining what you see. You must discipline the movies you watch, discipline what you look at on the Internet, and discipline the kinds of things you read.

**The eyes of the wise stay focused and alert.**

Proverbs 4:25-26 says:

> *Let your eyes look straight ahead, and your eyelids look right before you. Ponder the path of your feet, and let all your ways be established.*

Look straight ahead of you. Let your eyelids look at what is right before you; focus on what is in front of you and not on what somebody else is doing. Don't even look at what is behind you, or to your left or right. Focus on what you are doing; focus on your assignment; focus on your purpose. Don't look at another person's life and try to be like them. You don't know where they are going and where they'll end. Focus on what is right ahead of you, in front of you and the steps you are taking, so you don't fall. That is where your eyes must be.

Sometimes we get too distracted in life, looking at other people and we become very unhappy with what God has blessed us with. Many times the dissatisfaction we have in life is not based on what we don't have; it is based on what other people have. It's almost like you are working and you are earning five hundred cedis[7], and you are fine. You live on the five hundred cedis, and then you hear that somebody else earns six hundred cedis, then all of a sudden, you are not fine with your salary. The problem is not the money; the problem is your focus. You are focusing wrongly and when you are focusing wrongly, you will never be happy with your life.

You know there are people who are married who are not happy with the person they married? There are women who are not happy with their husbands. They look at their husbands and say, 'look at that man', but they fell in love with him, whatever 'that' is, they fell in love with it and they were okay until they saw somebody else who dresses differently, or talks differently and all of a sudden, she despises who she once wanted more than anyone else.

There are men who look at their wives and say 'look at my wife, look at her'. But you fell in love with her. There are probably about 3.5 billion women on this planet. You fell in love with one. That's your choice and if you keep your eyes on what you have you will not be side-tracked. Another woman may look different, but do you know their problems too? Keep your eyes focused, and yes, God will bless you. God can bless you financially, revive your marriage and give you more, but until He gives you more, focus on what you have.

If you have only one pair of shoes, be grateful. If you have two, be grateful. If you have ten, be grateful. If you have twenty, be grateful.

## The Face of the Wise

You can tell a lot about people by looking at their face. You can look at somebody's face and tell that they are worried and unhappy. You can look at somebody's face and know that he's broke. When people are broke their face has a different kind of look. You can look at somebody's face and know that things are going well for him. So how does a wise person's face look like? Can you look at a person and see that he's not wise? Ecclesiastes 8:1 tells us what a wise face looks like:

> Who is like a wise man? And who knows the interpretation of a thing?
>
> A man's wisdom makes his face shine, and the sternness of his face is changed.

The New International version says:

> Who is like a wise man? And who knows the interpretation of a thing?
>
> Wisdom brightens a man's face and changes its hard appearance.

So when you see a person with a hard face, his wisdom is not manifesting.

### *A wise face inspires trust and confidence.*

A wise person normally is able to solve problems. They are able to interpret a thing, according to the passage. People who are able to solve problems, who can think through problems don't seem overwhelmed by problems. So although things may be hard and life may be difficult they always have a sense they can unravel it. They have a face that looks confident. That's a wise man's face.

They don't look perplexed, confused, overwhelmed and not knowing what to do. There are people who look shocked all the time. Always, their eyes are big, and you look at their face and know that wisdom is lacking.

But there are other people that you talk to them about a problem and they listen. They say, *is that so? So what can we do about it?* You just look at his face, and you, looking at them, feel confident because it is a wise man's face, he knows how to solve a problem; he knows how to unravel a riddle; he knows how to dismantle a crisis; and he knows how to order his life. A wise man's face is always inspiring trust and confidence.

Have you ever been to a place where you have an uncle or somebody you know there, and you know this person is wise? Anytime they are around you, you feel at peace. When you go to their home, you know that you will never leave with a problem. You are going to have a solution; you are going to have a perspective that will help you. A wise man's face is like that.

### *A wise face glows with honour and character.*

Secondly, the wise man's face glows; it is bright with honour and character. When a person is wise their face becomes honourable and weighty. You see the person's face; it is heavy. You cannot just talk anyway to the person. You are careful not to expose your own lack of wisdom. The wise man's face glows.

If people feel comfortable just rambling to you, I just want to advise you that something is lacking. If anybody anywhere can get up and talk to you roughly, vulgarly and disrespectfully, not thinking about what they say to you, then you need a face upgrade because when you are wise, your face must not be easy for people to insult and downgrade because a wise man's face has honour and character. They may do it when you are not there, but right in your face, they cannot do it because your face has honour and character.

So, do you have a wise man's face? I don't know. I know I'm trying to develop one. Do you have a wise man's eye? Do you have the lips of the wise? When you talk, do people say, *oh, that's a wise person*? Do you have the ears of the wise? Do you seek knowledge, and are you able to handle rebuke? Do you have the heart of the wise? These are good questions to ask yourself sometime. They are a way to check which direction you are going, a way to check your growth, and a way to check your wisdom.

I believe each one of us can be people of wisdom. Nobody is born with wisdom; wisdom is acquired. We can learn; we can walk in wisdom and if we are going to be people of wisdom, it will have to be with the right heart; it will have to be with the right ears. If we are going to be wise people, then our lips must say the right things.

Our eyes must see the right things; and our faces must shine with the glow of wisdom. May God help us to develop wisdom in our lives.

CHAPTER

## 08

# HOW TO GET WISDOM

I know that we have looked at dimensions, functions, types, contrasts, the source, the excellence and examples of wisdom, perhaps we should ask, *is wisdom for everyone? Is it reserved only for special people? Do I already have it? And if not, how do I get wisdom?* Proverbs 4:5-9 answers many of these questions in no uncertain terms. It reads,

> *Get wisdom! Get understanding! Do not forget, nor turn away from the words of my mouth. Do not forsake her, and she will preserve you; love her, and she will keep you. Wisdom is the principal thing; therefore get wisdom. And in all your getting, get understanding. Exalt her, and she will promote you; she will bring you honour, when you embrace her. She will place on your head an ornament of grace; a crown of glory she will deliver to you.*

These are very powerful phrases about wisdom. In this passage, again wisdom has a feminine description and is presented as a woman. I stated in chapter two that the reason is to show the desirability of wisdom and to signal to us that we should go after wisdom the same way a man goes after a woman he loves. It uses that analogy to shape our attitude about wisdom.

If the Bible tells us to get wisdom in all our getting, it presupposes that it is possible to get wisdom, and it is not an unattainable virtue that can only be acquired by special people. Everybody can get wisdom, and if we want to perform beyond our current level, our wisdom capacity must expand so we can mature up to it.

## Attracting Wisdom

What then should be our attitude towards wisdom? Proverbs 4:5-9, tell us how wisdom should be treated to draw it into your life. There are five things to do to attract wisdom.

- **Pursue her**. The proverb says you should get wisdom. This means to passionately pursue it. Wisdom must not be pursued passively. The image here is of a man who has seen the lady of his dreams and goes all out to win her heart. Usually, in the natural world it is called "the chase." When a man goes after a woman he is said to be chasing after her, not crawling after her. It means there is urgency to his pursuit. Those who are married will understand this wisdom better. When a man falls in love, he dreams about the lady, plans his moves to win her affection, and his heart beats faster when he sees her. A man in love will make all kinds of excuses to see her. He will conveniently position himself where he knows she'll pass.

  The Bible says this is how wisdom should be treated; you

should conveniently put yourself in the place where wisdom is passing. When wisdom is seen or heard anywhere, your heart should quicken. You should be passionate to get it. You cannot be passive about wisdom and decide to get it when you have time. No, you should be dreaming about it, thinking about it; it should occupy your mind and your heart should beat fast for it. You must have a real passion for wisdom.

- **Love her.** Next, the Bible says to love wisdom. This means care deeply for wisdom. When you have pursued and acquired her, don't lose interest in her. Pay attention and spend time with wisdom. Talk about wisdom. If you love wisdom, she will love you back, so love her.

- **Exalt her.** The Scripture says we must exalt wisdom. This means give wisdom a high value. Prioritize wisdom. Wisdom should be exalted above money, above material wealth and above power.

- **Remember her.** We must also remember wisdom. This means to always keep wisdom in your mind. Do not allow time and age to diminish your love for wisdom. One of the most beautiful sights in our world is that of an old man and woman who have been in love for probably sixty years and still walking in love and talking with endearment.

- **Be loyal to her.** And finally we must not forsake wisdom. This means do not exchange wisdom for anything. You may be tempted to exchange wisdom for something else, but do not fall for it.

## Wisdom is worth more than money, power or fame.

Wisdom faces a lot of competition and one of its greatest competitors is money. Running close behind money in the competition with wisdom is power and fame. Money, power and fame are good in the right context, but if you acquire them without wisdom you become a liability and a menace to yourself.

That was the problem with King Solomon. He had wisdom but he forsook wisdom and began to pursue power, fame and women. He was not in love with all the women he married; he married them for political expediency. He wanted to form alliances with his neighbours and for the sake of peace he married women from different tribes. He pursued power at the expense of wisdom. So sometimes we have wisdom but we forfeit it to pursue other things.

The Bible says wisdom is the principal thing to acquire. It is the most important pursuit of your life and in all the things that you may get in life; you should be determined to get wisdom and understanding. Don't seek money first; seek wisdom. Don't desire power first; desire wisdom. Don't pursue fame first; pursue wisdom. The Bible says, in all your getting, get wisdom. The number one pursuit of our lives shouldn't be greatness, popularity or wealth; it should be wisdom.

Since the Bible places so much emphasis on getting wisdom, then we must be intentional about getting it. We must pursue and intensely look for it, to exalt wisdom so wisdom will exalt us; and if we forget wisdom, wisdom will forget us. It is like a courtship. We must attract wisdom to want to be with us. In the next section I want us to look at how, once we have attracted wisdom to come close to us, how do we secure her so that she will stay? Let's look at seven ways the Bible tells us how to have and to hold onto wisdom.

## Seven Ways to Get Wisdom

### 1. The fear of the Lord.

The first way to get wisdom is very obvious. If you want to be wise you should start at the very beginning – the fear of the Lord. Proverbs 9:10 says,

> *The fear of the LORD is the beginning of wisdom, and the knowledge of the Holy One is understanding.*

Wisdom starts with an acknowledgement of God as the source of wisdom in our lives. To have wisdom we have to realize that we are not our own creators; that there is Somebody above us, who made us and to whom we are accountable. The fear of the Lord means having reverence for God; it means having respect for God and to honour the things of God. Wisdom starts with the fear of the Lord. If you miss that, you cannot get wisdom.

### 2. Listening and learning.

The second way to get wisdom is by listening and learning. It is very difficult to get wisdom if you are not good at listening. Proverbs 1:5 says,

> *A wise man will hear and increase learning, and a man of understanding will attain wise counsel.*

This is how Solomon started his journey of wisdom. If you read Proverbs 1, he tells us that he got his wisdom from listening and learning from his Father. He listened and learned long before he later prayed for wisdom. The prayer is not what began his path to attaining wisdom; the wisdom started by listening and learning.

We find the same example with Jesus. At just twelve years old, Jesus spent time in the temple listening to older people. Was He the Son of God? Yes. Was He the Redeemer? Yes. He was actually the creator of the people He was talking to, but He showed us that if you are going to be wise, it doesn't start by talking; you start by listening. Wisdom doesn't enter through the mouth; it enters through the ears. Although Jesus was just twelve years old, He could have stood in front of all those priests in the temple and said, hey, don't you know whom I am? I am Jesus, the Son of the Living God. I created the heavens and the earth, and I'm here to teach you, but Jesus, as a human, showed us the way we humans must go about things. If you are going to be wise in this world you start by listening. Solomon also knew to start by listening. If Jesus said you start by listening, and Solomon also said you start by listening, then we should follow their lead, and start our pursuit of wisdom by listening.

I have never seen anyone become wise who doesn't listen. Listening introduces you to ideas. Wisdom is gained by observing and learning from the things that happen around you, but if you are the type of person who get tired of listening and cannot be bothered with observing and evaluating, you will never be wise.

### 3. Befriend the wise.

The third path to wisdom is to make friends with wise people. Proverbs 13:20 says,

> *He who walks with wise men will be wise, but the companion of fools will be destroyed.*

It makes sense. If you respect the Lord, who is the source of wisdom, and you are keen to listen and learn, then it makes sense that being around wise people will increase your wisdom. If you watch a wise person, you will pick up some of their wisdom. If you ask questions from a wise person, they will share their wisdom. If a wise person observes you and comments on what you are doing, you will gain some of their wisdom.

So just ask yourself, *Am I a companion of fools or do I walk with the wise?* Do an audit of your friends. Don't tell them; do it quietly. Look at the ten people closest to you. Think of or even list the ten people whose advice you listen to, or whom you bounce off ideas with. Now ask the question, *do I keep wise company and wise counsel?*

Young people, if you are going to marry, who are the people you will consult and say, *listen, I've seen this lady I want to marry, or listen, I've seen this man I want to marry, what do you think?* Who are those people? Write down their names and evaluate; are they wise, or are they foolish? What kind of marriage do they have? How wisely have they chosen?

If you are a businessperson preparing to make an investment, who are the top people you are going to talk to? Make a list of them; taking note of the people whose opinion you seek and the people who advice you. Do an audit of the quality of advice they've given you so far. Whose advice gets you into trouble and whose advice has led you to success? Those whose advice always creates more problems for you may be nice looking, they may mean well, they may be your closest friends, but they are not wise. As harsh as this may sound, if you continue to keep fools in your close circle, you are headed towards becoming one of them, as the saying goes; you become the company you keep.

Remember the story of Solomon's son, Rehoboam? Rehoboam was the child of a wise man, but he was one of the most unwise kings of Israel. Once when he was going to make a decision, he consulted the companions of his father, Solomon, who advised him on how to manage the country. They told him to lower taxes so that life would be easier for the people and they would love him. Then he decided to seek a second opinion from his friends who advise him to be hard on the people so they would respect his power. He went with his friends' advice, and after he came down with an iron fist on them, everybody left him to govern only himself. From that time the kingdom was split into two. Second opinions are not always right.

Be sure to make friends with wise people. If you know somebody who is wise, get close to the person, and don't make decisions without consulting somebody you see to be wise. The Bible says, in the multitude of counselors, there is safety. It doesn't say in the multitude of counsel8. It says, counselors. There are people who give counsel who are not counselors. Don't just look for a multitude of advice because a multitude of bad advice will not keep you safe. Just because ten unwise people give you similar advice, does not mean that the multitude of their advice will turn into wisdom. It is the quality of the advice, determined by the quality of the person advising you that gives you the safety. How many counselors are in your life? And I'm not talking about how many people offer you their opinion, but how many of them are counselors?

If you have a marriage problem and you go and talk to somebody who himself cannot manage his own marriage, then you are putting your marriage in danger not safety. It is logical that you wish to talk to your father about your problem. You say, daddy, my wife is giving me problems and this marriage *is hard*. Your father says, *don't worry, that's how women are. You come, I will show you how I dealt with all the women, including your mother. I will show you.* Yes he is your father and in the ideal world, a father should be a good counselor, but your observation of his treatment of your mother tells you that he's not the ideal husband. He may advise you, but you should be most concerned with whether he is a counselor? He may have old age, but what is the quality of his experience? The only way his advice could become qualitative for you is if he tells you *this is what I did and failed, so don't do what I did.* But if he recommends his failure to you, have the strength of character to reject it. It may be your mother, father, aunt or even your pastor, because, and I wish it were not so, but not all pastors are wise. I don't criticize other pastors, so this is not about a specific person, but generally speaking, not all pastors are wise. Some are good preachers, but have some wisdom problems. Just be mindful to make friends with the wise because, as the Scripture says, *he who walks with wise men will be wise, but the companions of fools will be destroyed.*

**4. Receive correction and amend.**

The fourth way to get wisdom is to receive correction and make amends. One of the best ways to be wise is to be open to correction. Proverbs 15:31-32 says,

> *The ear that hears the rebukes of life will abide among the wise. He who disdains instruction despises his own soul, but he who heeds rebuke gets understanding.*

Verse 31 tells us that sometimes life will rebuke you. That's when life whips you. Wisdom is determined by whether or not you learn from it. You don't become wiser from the hard lessons you experience. You become wiser by what you take from them.

Sometimes, you will make a decision and it will come back and smack you. You say to yourself, *wow, I thought I was right, but the repercussion is bad!* That's a rebuke of life. Perhaps you made an investment. Somebody promised you that if you invest in this thing, in two years it will multiply and then you can solve all your financial problems, but instead those two years whipped you. It is called the rebuke of life. Maybe you had an opportunity and you destroyed it. That is painful. It's the rebuke of life; and there are some people who never hear the rebukes of life. Life whips them but they don't hear. When life smacks you and you don't learn, it will smack you again and again. Some people are rebuked by life but they never learn; they continue to make the same mistakes.

You will sometimes see people who have married seven times. If it didn't work on the fourth marriage it means you are making the same mistakes. The problem is the people you are choosing, and somewhere in there, the problem is you. Life is slapping you but you are not learning. *The ears that hear the rebukes of life will abide among the wise.* So when life rebukes you, learn. Don't turn every correction into an attack. Don't say *the devil is attacking me; the devil is a liar.* Instead accept that *life is rebuking me and life tells the truth.* Make amends and correct yourself and you will be wise.

I remember talking to an older mentor of mine; he's a pastor, and he's now about ninety years old, and still preaching. Almost twenty years ago, he told me of a time when he was travelling, sometime in the forties, and he was going to take a train. As he was on his way to buy the ticket, somebody picked his money from his pocket. He said after that, he never put money in his pocket, and he told me where he puts his money instead. I won't tell you that, but he said he learnt from that experience not to put money in his pocket again. It's called the rebuke of life. He received the correction and changed his practices.

**5. Guard your emotions and your words.**

The fifth way to get wisdom is by guarding your emotions and your tongue. We all know that wise people are not frantic and they don't speak recklessly. Proverbs 17:27-28 says,

> *He who has knowledge spares his words, and a man of understanding is of a calm spirit. Even a fool is counted wise when he holds his peace; when he shuts his lips, he is considered perceptive.*

It is wise to learn quietness. We have to learn to shut our lips, like the verse says. Control the urge to speak all the time. Control the urge to be hurt and angry all the time. Develop a calm spirit; don't be hasty in your responses to life. Control the urge to panic when things are not going well. Things may not go well, but don't panic. Don't jump out of the frying pan, because you will land in the fire. At least you are accustomed to the frying pan; so before you jump out make sure you are aware of where you are landing.

I remember years ago, there was fire in our home, and I was in the shower having my bath, and the fire started in the sitting room. I heard shouts 'fire, fire, fire, come out.' And I said, 'come out to do what?' I had to quickly assess what to do. Sure, there was a fire, but after the fire has been put out, everybody will remember. I advised myself with a calm spirit. I didn't panic; I didn't jump. Don't just respond because things are hard. Guard your emotions and your tongue.

### 6. Appreciate the brevity of life.

The sixth way to get wisdom is to appreciate the brevity of life. Psalms 90:12 says,

> *So teach us to number our days, that we may gain a heart of wisdom.*

When we are young we see ourselves as having a lot of time. We look ahead of us and wonder when will we ever grow. Those above fifty and sixty years can recall saying, *Oh, I want to grow up; I want to grow up*. Now I am sure they want to be young. Look at all the things they are doing – dyeing the hair, and trying to do all kinds of things just to be young. They were the ones who wanted to grow old, now their hair is grey and they want to dye it.

As you grow older, you realize how short life is. When I was young and heard somebody was seventy, I wondered, 'eh, a human being! How can you be seventy!' Now, seventy is just around the corner – whether I like it or not. I can bind it, rebuke it in the Name of Jesus, reject it, resist it, command it by the blood of the Lamb, but I will still be growing. So the Bible says, *teach us to number our days that we may apply our hearts to wisdom.*

Have a practice of adding twenty years to your age all the time and you will be wise. Almost instantly, wisdom will hit you. That is when you start panicking and thinking, *I don't have this; I haven't done this; I haven't done that*. Because until you see that time is short you will not appreciate the important things of life.

You may grow to be seventy, you may grow to be eighty or ninety. Now all of that seem short to me. Life may even take you to a hundred and twenty years, but it is still short. No matter how long you prolong it, it is still short. So teach us to number our days that we may apply our hearts to wisdom.

When you start numbering your days, you will appreciate every moment God gives you. You will appreciate life. You will appreciate the fact that you can get up from bed and walk out; you will appreciate the fact that you can put your own clothes on your body, because some people cannot. You can appreciate when you wake up in the morning and you are alive; the birds are singing; you say 'wow, I made it another day,' and apply your heart to wisdom. Because every day the clock ticks, you've lost something that you can never gain again. You will never regain yesterday. You will never regain last year ever again. You will never have this moment again; it is past. And if you don't utilize it, it will just add grey hair to you, but not quality. Be mindful of days.

Those of you who are young don't take it for granted. Not too long ago, we were all young. We were all about twenty-five and talking about 'we'll take the world; we'll take the world.' Now, thirty years later, you wonder, how much of the world have you taken? 'Teach us to number our days that we may apply our hearts to wisdom.' Those of you who are young, whatever you have to do, do it wisely. Don't make too many mistakes in life; don't spend the bulk of your life correcting your mistakes. Minimize your mistakes so your life will be more progressive than taking one step forward, two steps backwards to come and make amends.

For some of us, our lives are just about correcting mistakes and there is no progress. The older you grow the fewer mistakes you should make. The older you grow, you have to be more thoughtful and deliberate. Minimize your mistakes because if you are making mistakes at sixty, when are you going to correct them? If you are making mistakes at fifty, when will you correct them? You may not have time to correct them. One of the things you realize is that when you are young life is more flexible. Little children fall down on the floor and get up; sometimes they fall by themselves and get up, then they laugh.

One of the things I didn't understand when I was growing up was when I heard my older aunties talking about somebody older who fell down, maybe while taking his bath. I used to think 'he should get up.' I didn't know that when you are older and you fall, you don't get up, because as you grow older when you fall, it is more difficult to bounce back; more difficult to recover, so you have to minimize your falling; you have to minimize your mistakes because recovery is going to take you a long time.

Some men are sixty-five years and they've now gone for a girl. After all the wisdom you've accumulated in your life, you now have a twenty-five-year-old girl by your side. Okay, it is your wisdom; you follow it; it is a free world so you follow it. 'Teach us to number our days.'

### 7. Pray for wisdom.

The final way to get wisdom is to pray for wisdom. James 1:5 says,

> *If any of you lacks wisdom, let him ask of God, who gives to all liberally and without reproach, and it will be given him.*

In other words, if points 1 to 6 have failed, then pray. Ask God to give you wisdom. And in addition to points 1 to 6, pray. Praying for wisdom is not a one-time activity. Praying for wisdom is seeking God's wisdom in all the major choices of your life. It is a daily, moment-by- moment activity.

Somebody is speaking to you, and you are heating up getting angry. When you are getting angry, you will see it. What the person is saying to you is really making you angry and getting very bad by the minute. At that time, pray for wisdom. Say 'Lord, I'm getting angry, I'm heating up, give me wisdom.' Somebody is making you a financial offer; pray for wisdom. Somebody has told you something; pray for wisdom.

You've just discovered a secret; pray for wisdom. You heard something that somebody spoke about you, pray for wisdom.

If we are constantly praying for wisdom, constantly, the inspiration of the Almighty will give us understanding. And sometimes in that moment of vulnerability, God just calms your spirit and the anger just evaporates or the panic evaporates, or the fear evaporates.

Pray for wisdom all the time. One of the practices I've developed for years is to pray for wisdom. I pray for wisdom more than anything in my life. I pray for wisdom constantly. Even when I'm preaching, I'm praying for wisdom. Constantly. 'Lord, help me; Lord, give me wisdom; Lord, help me understand; Lord, open my mind, open my heart, Lord, teach me', constantly, because one moment you will slip and that slip may give you a bad fall. One moment you will make a mistake that you will never be able to repair for the rest of your life. So ask God for wisdom.

And the Bible says, that's the good news; that He gives to all liberally. In other words, when you pray for wisdom God will breathe wisdom into you, but remember, it is the breath of the Almighty; not the wind; it is going to be a breath. You pray for wisdom and He breathes an idea to you; He calms your spirit and He leads you. Don't harden your heart; receive the breath of the Almighty that He will protect and preserve you.

CHAPTER

## 09

# PRAYING FOR WISDOM

If, after reading this book you feel you haven't been wise, the good news is that there is grace and hope for you. You can change. You can make new responses in life. Be a bit more investigative and begin to ask questions. Look a little further beyond the surface and dig deeper until you reach solid ground. Accept, embrace and work with realities instead of denying them in your heart. When you adopt these attitudes you will become wise.

As we make important choices in our lives - about career, marriage, money and most importantly, our eternal destination, may God help us to make wise decisions. By far, one of the best ways to receive God's help is to pray for it, so to conclude our journey on wisdom, here are a few prayer points you can offer up to God, to ask Him for wisdom. Remember, every problem you face is a wisdom problem, so indeed it is wise to ask God to grant you more wisdom.

## First, thank God that the wisdom of Christ is available to you.

Thank God for the incarnation of Jesus; thank God that He became man; thank God that He lived among us and that He died for us; thank God that He reconciled us unto Himself.

> *I thank you Lord. Thank you, Jesus, for becoming my wisdom, thank you that you are available to me; thank you that I can tap into your wisdom; thank you that I can reach spiritually into you and receive wisdom for every area of my life. Thank you, Father, for freely availing wisdom to me. In you I have access to wisdom. In you I have access to clarity of thought. In you I have access to knowledge revelation, and illumination. Lord, I thank you that you didn't leave me in my ignorance, but you come to me with knowledge, with understanding, with clarity. I give you praise, Lord, I you give you adoration, I thank you for the wisdom that is available to me.*

## Ask God to open your eyes to every area of your life where you lack wisdom.

In each one of us there are areas in our lives where we lack wisdom. If you examine yourself you will know that in a particular area you lack wisdom, you don't handle things well in that area of your life. Pray and ask God to open your eyes to every area of your life where you lack wisdom. Say,

> *Lord, open my eyes to my own weaknesses, to my own failings, to my own limitations and to my own lack of knowledge. Help me, Lord, to know times when I sabotage my own self. Help me Lord to know the things I do that continue to give me defeat. Make me aware of my own weakness.*

## Ask God for wisdom in a specific area of your life.

Name it and say,

*Lord, I ask you for wisdom. In this area of my life where I make the wrong decisions, I ask you for wisdom, Lord. I ask you for wisdom for my marriage, for my children, for my business, I ask you for wisdom for my health, I ask you for wisdom for my career. Lord, Your Word says if we lack anything, ask and You will give it to us. Lord, give me wisdom. Help me not to be a destroyer. Lord, help me not to be one who pulls down, but make me a person of wisdom. Help me Lord to be a preserver, help me to lift up and to build.*

**Ask the Lord to enlighten the eyes of your understanding to know the hidden treasures He has put in you.**

The apostle Paul prayed, asking that the eyes of our understanding may be enlightened that we may know the riches of His glory in our lives. There is something in you that you don't know. There are things in you that you haven't discovered yet. Your teacher didn't discover them, your parents haven't discovered them and nobody has ever seen them but they are in you, they are hidden treasures. Ask God to reveal to you and open your understanding to everything He has put in you that you haven't realized yet. Ask Him to show you the abilities, talents, gifts, uniqueness, strengths and opportunities He has made available to you. Ask to know yourself the way that God knows you. Just say,

*Lord open my eyes to see the deep treasure that you have given to me, to see the ability you have endowed me with. Grant me the wisdom to see the talents you have given to me. Open my eyes to see the paths that are opening for me. Help me Lord to know myself better. Help me to understand myself better. I want to know myself the way You know me, Lord. May every hidden treasure in me be discovered now in the name of Jesus. Father, help me to walk in wisdom, not in ignorance, not in foolishness. Help me to have your understanding of my*

> *strengths, understanding of my gifts, understanding of my uniqueness, understanding of my ability, understanding of the opportunity available to me, understanding of everything You have invested in me, in the name of Jesus.*

## Ask God to give you spiritual wisdom and understanding when you read the Bible.

The Scripture says *the entrance of God's word is light.* Pray that God will give you spiritual understanding when you read the Bible, because that is where He is going to guide you with wisdom. Many times when you read the Bible, many of us get tired, we get bored, we don't understand it, it is tiresome, and nothing comes to us. I want you to pray that God will make His word sweeter than honey to you, that anytime you study the word of God, sweetness will come out, that you will enjoy the Word. You will never be bored and the Scripture will come alive, that His word will speak to you, that His light will be imparted to you. Pray, for wisdom and understanding of the word of God. Ask for revelation of God's word, a deeper understanding of the Bible. Say,

> *Thank you, Lord, that the entrance of your word gives light. Let your word be sweet to my soul. Let me enjoy the richness of your word. Let your word be life to me. Let your word be living bread and living water to my soul. Let your word, oh God, refresh me and renew me. Oh God, open my eyes that I may behold wonders out of your word. In the name of Jesus, let the Bible come alive, let the word of God come alive to me. Grant me the spirit of wisdom and revelation in the knowledge of You. May every book of the Bible from Genesis to Revelation come alive to me.*

## Ask the Holy Spirit to be your counselor, teacher, guide and helper.

Jesus told His disciples, *It is expedient, it is right that I go away because when I go, the Holy Spirit will come and when He comes He will lead you into all truth. He will remind you of things I have spoken to you about. He will be your teacher, He will be your counselor, and He will be your helper.* Talk to the Holy Spirit and say,

> *Holy Spirit be my counselor. From today I receive you as my teacher, as my helper and as my guide. Show me what to do, help me, walk with me, and move with me in every area of my life. Be my counselor. Give me good counsel. Give me good advice. Give me good direction. Oh, Holy Spirit be my wisdom. Direct me and order my steps. Help me to discern your leading and your guidance, in Jesus name.*

## Ask for wisdom beyond your age, education and beyond your time.

The wisdom that God gives to us is beyond our age. God's wisdom is beyond your education. God's wisdom is beyond your experience. God does not give you wisdom equivalent to your age, to your education or to your experience. Jesus was 12 years old when He sat with religious professors in the temple and amazed them with His wisdom. He was not old, He was not educated, and He was not experienced. The wisdom that God pours into our heart is not based on age, experience and education. God is able to make you wiser than your education, wiser than your age, wiser than your experience. So ask Him,

> *Lord, make me wiser than my education, make me wiser than my age, and make me wiser than my experience. Whatever I have known in the past, give me wisdom surpassing that. What I have never read in a book, what I have never learned from anyone, what nobody has taught me, what nobody has exposed me to Lord, let your Spirit teach me. Help me Lord. In every*

*area of my life Lord, I ask for divine wisdom, divine wisdom beyond my time, beyond my age, beyond my experience. I give you glory, Lord.*

**Ask God to make you ten times better.**

When God gave Daniel and the other Hebrew children wisdom, the Bible says they were tested and they were 10 times better. May God make you ten times better. Pray and ask Him. Say,

*Father, do in me what I cannot do for myself Lord. Make me better Father. Like Daniel and the Hebrew children Lord, make me 10 times better. Make me 10 times better than my father Lord. Ten times better than my mother. Help me to be 10 times better that what I can be on my own Lord. Make me 10 times better for your glory, Lord. Grant me wisdom Father. Let your wisdom shine through me Lord. Ten times better, oh God. In the name of Jesus.*

If you have prayed these prayers with sincerity in your heart, I believe the Lord has heard you and He will answer your prayer. Cherish the wisdom He imparts in you. Never turn your back on it. Always seek it. No matter what else you attain in life, make sure you are always looking for wisdom. God bless you.

# ENDNOTES

[1] New Oxford American Dictionary (Second Edition).

[2] Mark 8:36

[3] Proverbs 4:5

[4] Agle, D. C.; Webster, Guy; Brown, Dwayne; Bauer, Markus (12 November 2014). "Rosetta's 'Philae' Makes Historic First Landing on a Comet." https://www.jpl.nasa.gov/news/news.php?release=2014-394NASA. Retrieved 11 October 2018.

[5] 1 Corinthians 1:30

[6] 2 Corinthians 5:17

[7] Ghanaian currency

[8] Proverbs 11:14